Wildwitch
The Craft of the Natural Psychic

Poppy Palin

Wildwitch
The Craft of the Natural Psychic

©1999 Poppy Palin

ISBN 186163 103 0

Cover design by Paul Mason
Cover and internal illustrations by Poppy Palin

Published by:

Capall Bann Publishing
Freshfields
Chieveley
Berks
RG20 8TF

By the same author, also from Capall Bann:

Season of Sorcery - On Becoming A Wisewoman

About the Author

Poppy Palin is a qualified and experienced artist whose work has appeared on greetings cards and in magazines. Although primarily an illustrator, Poppy also runs a tattoo studio. As a skin-artist Poppy specialises in esoteric imagery and treats tattooing as a spiritually based sacred art. Her tattooing has been used in ritual and to mark peoples' spiritual journeys.

WILDWITCH is Poppy's second book. Her first, SEASON OF SORCERY (Capall Bann, 1998) tells the story of her own life as a natural psychic. She is currently working on fiction books with broadly Pagan spiritual themes and considers herself to be a creative writer as much as an artist.

Poppy has also had experience as a teacher, a carer and a counsellor. Her background of working with people has enabled her to communicate more effectively as a psychic. She offers guidance and psychic readings to anyone in need of specific spiritual help.

Poppy lives with her growing menagerie of creatures in Wiltshire. Her hopes for herself are that she learns to accept the challenge of Motherhood, to fully experience the wonders of incarnating into female form. She would also like to be able to grow a decent organic vegetable!

I was born with the Seeing and the Knowing. I love these gifts as I love my own nature. I am part of all nature and my way is natural. I am a Wildwitch, my Craft is of the Wild. Here are my truths that they may help and inspire you to discover new ways of finding your own. Find your stars and walk your path in peace. Be wise, be wild, be blessed.

Contents

Foreword

'Wildwitch' is written from a perspective which holds the principle of reincarnation as one of the pivotal concepts of psychic work and Witchery. It therefore incorporates the past-life memories and experiences of the author, as well as other relevant people, into the text. The text itself is primarily concerned with the spiritual growth and development of the individual. The information is presented in a manner which assumes that reincarnation holds a key to individual self-knowledge and consequently universal understanding. Not all contemporary Witches believe this to be so and this book does not advocate the adoption of another individual's beliefs, wholesale. It does however suggest that looking at past-lives may be valuable to the reader as part of his or her quest and it offers examples of how this may be so.

As the author is a working psychic, the work is focussed on the Witch as a natural sensitive, in touch with this world and the Otherworlds. This contact with other levels of being and consciousness, both personal and global, depends upon a working relationship with spirit Guides. 'Wildwitch' accepts the presence of the Guide as a matter of fact in everyone's manifest life and uses examples of these as par for the course. Our interaction with these beings is also a core element of the book, as is associated inner psychic work, astral travel and psychic questing. Again, not all Witches would deem this to be a fundamental part of practicing the Craft. 'Wildwitch' offers a vision which sees no delineation between the Witch and the psychic or sensitive. They are one and the same and therefore contact with other dimensions and beings is considered to be wholly a part of the Craft as looked at here.

'Wildwitch' hopes to offer an alternative view of what it means to be a Witch, a natural born Witch, being as nature intended. It sees being a Wildwitch as using the inherent powers, natural powers which lie inert in many of us, only partially glimpsed. These latent powers, our innate energies which are akin to those of the greatest, most awesome aspects of nature, can be accessed and awoken by such inner work with Guides and the Otherworlds. 'Wildwitch' is about an inherent way of being, a soul-type that cannot be emulated by those not made that way naturally. This book suggests that no amount of book-learning or study can make a Witch when the essential psychic spark is missing. Of course, not all Witches would agree with that!

'Wildwitch' is about a way of being, an organic creation which can be enhanced by an individual's hard work and understanding. The text is about a voyage of discovery that is ongoing and which will hopefully inspire a questing spirit. It is definitely not a book for those who already believe that they know exactly what it means to be a Witch. It is a book for those who wish to value what they already know and respect what has gone before but who are not afraid to question everything, even if it means challenging established viewpoints. It is a work for those who were born seeking, those who are not afraid to look even when others cannot, or will not, see. Those of us with the wilderness within are always searching. We lie awake in the darkness, on the edge of the void, wanting to understand, seeking a lasting peace. 'Wildwitch' is for those of us who are the Seers and the dreamers, the ones for whom life is not easy but full of voices and visions, sometimes of a great aching longing for something that perhaps once was, but is no more. For these people, the born psychics, the sensitives, the true Witches, there is no alternative way of being. There is no closing the door on the true, wild Self without disastrous consequences, like trying to stop the ocean tides, or plugging up a volcano. The energy will out, will express itself. 'Wildwitch' encourages celebration and positive participation and interaction with these energies. It also encourages acceptance of these flows. Acceptance which is different from blindly submitting and swallowing what we have previously been told. An acceptance born of greater understanding, a greater understanding borne of asking our own questions and consequently getting our own answers. Of getting our own idea of the webs of possibility and probability that spread out from our every thought, action and deed.

Being a Witch, a Wildwitch, is difficult, time consuming and demanding. It is not a path many would opt for if they had not been born onto it, it is not for everyone. Even if it is not for you, if you are not of the wild, then at least you will have opened your mind and tried a new way. By accepting that this way is not for you there has been learning and growth. There is no better learning than understanding further who you be, or who you will never be, naturally.

By the cycles of death and rebirth we may come to understand ourselves better and so be a more effective and sensitive communicator and contributor to the All. This is the prayer of the Wildwitch and if it harm none so mote it be.....

Find your own stars,

Poppy Palin, Wiltshire, 1998.

4

To two true Wildwitches in their gentle spirits...Sue and Alice.

Blessings to the Guides, for never letting me fall too far.

With thanks and respect to those who try to save the greenwood. To them I am indebted.

For anyone who cares to find the Wildwood Within and dance there with the Great God Pan under a Gypsy Moon.

Introduction

Waking the Witch...

The Craft of the Wild. Wildwitchery. I love the word Wildwitch, it leaps across the page for me, alive with its own vibration. Resonant with overtones of freedom, evoking the vibrancy of nature, the potency and the magic. Wildwitch is a strong personal title to go by, it suggests instinctual gifts combined with knowledge gained, nature and the individual inextricably linked. I feel the Wildwitch to be a powerful natural force.

Not so very long ago I would have flinched from such a title, even as it grabbed for me. I preferred the sedate title of Wisewoman. On reflection it was a name which did not suit me personally yet it was the nearest possible description I could adopt for myself without using the word Witch. I saw the word Witch to be an insulting term, due to my having been called a Witch in a past incarnation as a form of derision and ridicule. I did not wish to attract such insults in this life and so I chose the less provocative label of Wisewoman which sounded respectable and gentle. Even though I was clearly a Witch in thought, action and appearance I stayed by the Wisewoman's fire and put on my spiritual slippers. I thought that I would be safe in this way, I also thought that I would be taken more seriously. However, my adoption of the wrong title caused nothing but confusion.

Whenever I called myself a Wisewoman I was asked "what's that?" and more likely than not I'd have to resort to the title of 'White Witch' anyway! This made the exercise of trying to avoid the word Witch rather pointless and worse, I thought the term White Witch was far too twee and 'Disney'. It is a terminology favoured by the media which reinforces those horrible, simplistic stereotypes of 'light equals good and dark equals bad'. To the inquisitive but uninformed enquirer I had to portray myself as a 'good witch' so that I would not scare them off from finding out more about what I do. The bland term 'White Witch' at least stopped anyone from perceiving me as a ridiculous Hammer Horror character...but then, why did I care how I was perceived?

The use of such labels proved to be a most unsatisfactory solution. Nobody knew what a Wisewoman was or what she did. It sounded like an occupation entirely reserved for females and so alienated any interested men who may have approached me. Yet to have to fall back on 'White Witch' for clarification defeated the object of me rejecting the Witchy terminology in the first place. It was time for a rethink as a label has to be accurate, it is a very powerful thing indeed.

The truth was that neither myself or others saw the epitomy of a Wisewoman archetype when they looked at me and felt my energies. I looked and felt like a Witch although I continued to hide in the folds of a mantle which partially fitted me but did not entirely suit me. The Wisewoman title conjured up images of a venerable and mature woman sat peacefully dispensing wisdom and remedies. I desired the security and respect this figure evoked and so I tried to adopt her disguise, I wanted her mode of being to make me acceptable and unthreatening. As ever in my previous attempts to hide my true nature it caused nothing but confusion to myself and others who observed me. My true 'scent', my emanations on a subtle level, were that of the Witch. The title still held a lot of fear for me as when one is wrongly tormented and executed in the name of Witchcraft in a past life then the soul-scars run deep and there is much residual angst. All I wanted to be was some harmless little eccentric who 'dabbled a bit' and alarmed no one. The

Wisewoman label was my last-ditch attempt to declare to the world "I'm definitely not weird, honestly!" As a subconscious response to what happened to my soul before when it had been associated with the emotive word Witch it is understandable. By adopting the Wisewoman label I sought to find the closest possible description for who and what I was without actually using the word itself. I was trying to be the Wisewoman whilst being easily recognisable as another similar, yet different, thing. A Witch is indeed a Wisewoman amongst other myriad things, but a Wisewoman is not necessarily a Witch. I can liken this misuse of a title to an antiques restorer calling themselves an antiques dealer. It is a close approximation but it does not actually describe what they do particularly well and anyone observing them could see this to be so.

Using the wrong title is misleading to others and it effectively disempowers the true self. It appears that we are ashamed of who we truly are and that we have to conceal the real identity. In my case, I did it from a left-over fear of persecution, a terror deep within me of pain and torture for who I be. When masquerading as another, we make a statement on both the physical and the spiritual levels of denying the natural self, of saying that self is somehow inadequate or unacceptable. This is a damaging thing to do on a long term basis. I am sure that we can all relate to the use of 'personas' for certain tasks, we all use props and bravado on occasion, including the adoption of certain character traits that are not naturally our own. This can be to get us through a tricky situation that makes us nervous and is entirely understandable as it is an act brought about by insecurity or worry. I can therefore totally understand my own temporary adoption of another persona as it was primarily motivated by a past fear. My adoption of the Wisewoman label and all that goes with it was not too far away from the truth although it was not the truth. It was not damaging in the long term in the same way that borrowing the traits of someone that we admire for a business meeting is not essentially damaging to the psyche. The analysis of why we need to do these things is the interesting part and should not be overlooked as a tool for gaining insights into the self.

I cannot, then, see my calling myself a Wisewoman as a mistake. It afforded me the time to question who I really was. I was claiming that I had broken my old patterns and ways of relating when in fact I had not. It was ironic that I chose to do this proclaiming in the public arena by means of the title of the first book that I had published. It was as if I had to make a statement to society on a larger scale, that if I were to draw attention to myself by writing a book then it must be under the most innocuous of labels. As I had only relatively recently relived my past incarnations, including that of my fourteenth century Witch burning, the very real sense of personal fear was still strong in me. As I had had several lives of being persecuted it was almost instinct for me to wish to hide behind the 'fluffiest' spiritual guise possible. My soul's dark memories were totally real to me and very close to the surface although consciously I genuinely thought that I was the Wisewoman and that I no longer lived in fear of any kind. My age old ingrained terror of persecution for being simply myself made me hide from my true way of being. I had to take on board that I had chosen to incarnate in a reasonably tolerant and interested society and therefore had freedom to be myself in entirety. It does not matter today what anyone else thinks or feels as I cannot be tortured and killed for who I be. I no longer have to appease anyone by name or otherwise. That is why I needed a title that I could divulge with pride and no attendant explanation. I am a Wildwitch, that is who I be, today, tomorrow and always.

I can still honour the Wisewoman within myself without being a Wisewoman. This archetype is a difficult one to take on as it has a shadow side which can be hard to bear without the attendant wisdom and inner peace that one needs. The positive is that the Wisewoman is left to her gentle existence of healing and dispensing spiritual knowledge whereby the world comes to her door and then leaves her again to a solitary life of musing. The negative is depression, alienation from the world and mental illness. With age and experience and with the right soul-type, the Wisewoman can understand these shadows and deal with them as part of her learning process. I myself can see how the idea of being left alone appealed (after lives desiring to be left alone to be who I was) but I was all too susceptible to the flipside of introspection and gloom.

With the Wisewoman I share the dreams, the prophesies and the visions and I also share the need for space, freedom and time to work on the inner planes. However, I can observe that I lack the balance of a true Wisewoman to deal with the darkness of the solitary soul and to learn profound lessons from it. The temptation to adopt her lifestyle is great until I remember the responsibility of dealing with that isolation from the real world. Perhaps in years to come I will acquire more of her reflective stillness and ease but for now my energies are too strong to live in almost hermetic retreat. I can understand totally how my soul sees living in a kind of spiritual hiding as being the safest manner in which to exist. However, I must separate my real needs from the aspects of my soul that have been twisted and misshapen by pain in lives previous. Who was I before my soul became damaged thus? What was I before I was afraid to reveal myself?

When I look at myself inside and when I connect to my very essence in meditation, writing or artworks I come to the same place. I have discovered the key words of my eternal soul before that soul was brutalised. I imagined the words that I would have tattooed upon my skin or etched into my manifest self as the absolute synopsis of my eternal self. In finding these key words I could connect with myself as the Wildwitch. The words I found were 'spirit of freedom' or 'free spirit'. 'Free spirit' conjures up bright images of celebration and joy, of energy and true wildness. Not wildness in the sense of mindless rebellion but wildness as of the wild, being wild as the fox, owl or deer. It suggests our being who we be without any sense of restriction, just being. None could deny that a fox is a free spirit, without artifice, beautiful and natural. Yet there are those who find its untamed behaviour to be surplus to human requirements. Free spirits in life can often evoke feelings of envy, fear or even violence. For example, the gypsy, the hippy, the outlaw wolfshead and more latterly, the eco-warrior. These are just some of the names that inspire or instill prejudice. They are bright, bold and unstoppable forces standing up for all they hold dear and being who they be, naturally. They have also been reduced to caricatures of themselves, reduced to a joke image to be ridiculed. This is disempowerment.

The Witch fits into this list alongside the other free spirits and the Witch has also been discredited, disempowered. The Witch is now a popular image of a ludicrous pointy hatted, warty, big nosed crone, the likes of which has never been seen on earth. Her image runs riot at Halloween, infests books and cartoons and even jumps out of the graphics package on my computer. If those are Witches then they are so patently a joke that they cannot possibly exist in the real world! The repeal of the Witchcraft Act may not have been because the Witches deserved freedom of expression and belief like anyone else but rather because in our age of science and logic how could anything so patently ludicrous exist? Free spirits like Witches are not generally encouraged to grow and shine, their thinking and ways may be contagious and they must be effect-ively kept under control. As the fox is brutally ripped apart by hounds to 'control' its wildness, its freedom to roam and to be, so are the other free human spirits crushed by mockery and disinformation.

We no longer rip human beings apart to keep them from being different and free but we do see them belittled and ripped apart with words. So why indeed have an Act against Witchcraft when it can be made into such a laughable piece of whimsy that people will neither believe in it or be afraid of it? Like Queen Victoria denying the existence of lesbianism (in her eyes it was so unthinkable that it could not happen) mainstream society denies real Witches exist outside of the cartoon fantasy. Thus Witches have been neutralised with humour, no doubt a very cunning device, and made into a foolish standard image. To the masses , Witches have become invisible save for this loathsome popular interpretation. Yet for some reason there is still an underlying interest like something gradually awaking on the fringes of the populace and slowly spreading inwards. Some of the Spirit of the Wild lives within us all and perhaps in some it is time for it to awaken. Not everyone is a Wildwitch but perhaps more and more individuals will gain an interest and understanding in what Witches inherently do.We can only ask for respect and give it in return. By using our title with pride we effect change. We do not hide or pretend and we show our presence, quietly revealing that there is a truth which has nothing to do with warts or big noses. That is empowerment. Its energy effects the All.

When a biker gets on to her bike, she can be seen to be a biker. When an eco-warrior chains himself into his treehouse as the bailiffs come, he can be seen to be who he is. When an artist paints he is an artist and when a traveller goes by in a horse drawn covered wagon she is a gypsy. Yet what does the Witch do to show he or she is a Witch? They 'smell' wrong to the pack of society although it may not be clear as to why. A Witch generally keeps there views and beliefs to themselves unless asked with genuine interest, so they cannot be spotted by their talk of who they be and what they do. What is there that positively identifies the Witch archetype? Although a Witch cannot conceal their Witchiness as such, it is still something that is difficult to define. It is the free spirit, the natural and eternal soul of the wild, born not made, which can be perceived by others. This 'scent' my attract strongly or repel in equal measures but it cannot be ignored. Nor can it be concealed for long without the adverse affects of such an energy block being felt.

I would like to ask the reader to consider now what their own key is, where they are from and what is their image and way of being? Are you the reader of those wild places that are hidden from most? Do you feel born of the uncivilised and unrestrained forces of nature which are untouched by convention and expectation? Do you feel the raw, instinctive power of the wild calling you, haunting you with a nameless yearning, feel this intense power within and without? Consider the questions that I posed for myself and ask if you too may claim the title of Witch with a pride that comes of being only your true self?

I am not a traditional Witch and could not claim hearthrite with the hereditaries or the Gardnerians or the Hedges. I have no lineage of ancestral Craft teachings to go by nor do I have a lifetime of country folk-magic to go on. I was born in a town and I lived in cities so I am hardly your average village Witch. I live relatively rurally in adulthood by choice and indeed it was my soul's choice to be born into a town. I cannot lament that I was not raised on a farm or in a hamlet as no doubt I would not have learned the pertinent lessons of my soul if I had been. I am a genuine Witch yet I will never have that instinctive feel for the cycles of nature and the plants and animals thereof that a life-long country dweller has. I used to fight against this and do crash courses in herbal lore or tree identification, only to be frustrated that I could not easily recall all I had read when walking the trackways of the West. All the book learning I tried to cram in was focussed around the folk-magic of the rural people. Although I was deeply attracted to the idea of being a solitary Witch I knew I was not a Hedgewitch, the epitomy of the village Spellwife. Although I deeply respected this way and learned much from it, it said little to me about my life. Again I was trying to be a square peg in a round hole, as with my Wisewoman guise. I had to learn that being of the Wild was more to do with being as nature intended than knowing everything about nature. A healthy interest and deep love of nature was far more pleasing than once again trying to be the epitomy of the traditional village Wise One.

Most of the books on the Craft focussed strongly on this aspect, of this accepted traditional path. I knew that if I was to move on as a Witch then I must stop emulating and start celebrating my own way. And chances are that if this is my discovery that others will be in need of similar discoveries. I am writing this book to encourage and inspire those potential Wildwitches who at present feel a little lost. Nobody needs a label but in a time when people only know that we 'smell' different it is nice to know and to say who we be. I have no desire to start an alternative cult of the Craft with its own dogma and belief yet I do acknowledge the need for an alternative view for those who are natural born psychics who need a positive self image and name. I speak from the personal experience of being lost and to me the concept of a Wildwitch seemed a good enough place to start understanding my self. In this way I hope that it will act as a spiritual springboard for others. Certainly understanding and relating to the concept of Wildwitch I have here is not the end of the journey or quest, for me or for the reader.

To be a Wildwitch as I see it is to have a delight in the unknown, a thirst to learn and grow organically, a positivity and excitement about discovering spiritual truths. Wild-witchery is about genuinely accepting change and challenge with a glad heart and open mind. This is something which I have learned and it was the largest lesson of my incarnate life so far. It was my original basis for questioning everything as suddenly I had no choice but to do just that.

A year ago I would have denied any possibility of my being in the position I am in today. I have learned never to deny a possibility. My whole world has turned around in the space of a year, the wheel turned and I was in danger of not turning with it. I thankfully remained flexible even though it hurt to bend and I came through the trial. This valuable lesson forms the basis of this book...to be a Wildwitch is to go with the flow. The flow of natural energies be they universal or personal. We may not understand why the flow is such at this time, but we can be certain that the universe is unfolding as it should be. In time we will certainly gain understanding but for now we must work with the energies that are in everything and everyone. This includes gaining understanding of our own needs and ways. Just as I once learned that there is no point fighting against the energy I have to move objects 'poltergeist' style, I have now learned that all energy without exception must be worked with. We are far more effective when we work with that natural force without ignorance and, consequently, fear born thereof.

This book shares my story and those of others who have shared with me. The stories aim to bring greater understanding of how we may best work spiritually for the good of the All and they aim to stress the vital importance of working with the universal energy flow. It is a book which stresses the role of the natural psychic or Wildwitch as a psychic quester, one who helps other 'non-Witches' understand the energies at work in their own lives. The energies link us all to the All, with no exceptions. Working with the energies is a fascinating and endlessly enlightening experience. Hopefully, in terms of this work, the tales of how I worked with the webs and strands of life energy will also entertain.

To wake the Wildwitch within we must consider other possibilities and be prepared to walk into strange places alone. We must accept that we know that we truly do not know. We must hear and really listen. We must ask "what if?" and "why?" as we work with our own natural psychic rhythms and patterns. We should never underestimate our own personal, natural power and its effects on all that there is. When we grow spiritually, no matter how small that movement is, our place changes and we shift. Such a small movement displaces everything, change ripples on and on. From just one question as part of our personal questing we can effect countless changes, from that one element of growth and learning we make a difference.

We can all, each one of us, effect the All by thought and deed. The Wildwitch knows this and works with it. The late Linda MacCartney, animal rights supporter and creator of an innovative line of vegetarian cuisine, was quoted as saying "If I could save one animal!" before she began her work. From that one small thought, a prayer, the larger ripples were felt and her dream went on and on. Although Linda was unable to see all the animals that she had saved by her thoughts and deeds it did not make them any less real. Her husband, Sir Paul, said to her before she died "You've saved so many, millions of them, miles and miles and miles".

One does not need a famous husband or fame or wealth to create and to change. This example illustrates the personal power we all have and that the Wildwitch learns how to work with. We all have the power but the Wildwitch knows how it works and how to use it for the most harmonious outcome, through a spiritual overview.

We must never forget that a Wildwitch has the energies, the power, of nature. It is a Wild dance, for the brave and Wild at Heart, the reward being that we are being all we can be, true to ourselves and there is no better act of sacred worship than that. Not everyone can walk the path into the wilderness and not everyone would want to. It is hard work and it can be lonely. Remember when you read this that you are not alone in your spiritual work or on your questing journey. The quest is your own but the energies are shared. We all do our little bit and collectively the impact is felt. Everything is energies, our energies are everything.....

The Wheel turns and so we Become.

Chapter One
Going with the Flow

What a difference a year can make! In terms of my own life, some unbelievable changes have taken place which should have caused me untold unhappiness and discomfort. In this chapter, as with the others, I shall be drawing on my own personal experiences in order to make relevant points. This is not self-indulgence but merely a way of giving form to what could otherwise be a concept or idea which lacked any accompanying imagery to bring it to life. Many people are aided by imagining a picture to recall the text. I use a story, in the way that all spiritual workers have passed on sacred knowledge through the ages, rendering the subject more palatable and memorable by being entertaining, thus creating mind-pictures.

In this first instance, I wish to share the relevance, the paramount importance, of going with the cosmic flow. Although this phrase is seen today to be little more than a glib 'hippy-ism' tantamount to letting life, the universe and all wash over you whilst remaining in a lazy, apathetic state, it is in fact essential to spiritual well-being. It is not a case of letting life pass you by, letting anything and everything happen to you with a sense of uncaring inevitability. On the contrary, compared such inertia, it is vital to go with the flow in order to be fully awake to life's potential possibilities. It is about being alive to the energy flow that directs all life, our lives.

In order go with any universal flow we must have a means of interpreting it, a larger perspective than our own view. To

20

gain this overview of the energies which influence our life-patterns we need to speak with and listen to our spiritual Guides.

We all have Guides and they come in all manner of shades, shapes and sizes (as we shall see in another chapter.) What is vital is our acknowledgement of them and our subsequent communication with them as real beings, as integral parts of our lives. Only they can share with us the bigger picture needed to achieve a better understanding of the webs of possibility and only they can assist us with our energy flow.

As we are all of energy, constantly involved in complex exchanges with all life-forms and environments, we may either be compatible with the energies of another person or place, or not. More fundamentally, we can be in harmony with the flow of energy which is essential to our own lives, or not. We can block our own energies and cause stagnation, confusion and illness in our incarnations by not wishing to understand, and move with, the flow we should be following. Our Guides can point out to us where we may best move in the 'cosmic chess game' of existence as to best aid the flow and smooth transference of energies. We alone cannot do this.

As guidance from our spiritual mentors comes from the perspective of the 'bigger picture' we can trust that they oversee the patterns and threads that make up all lives. They may advise us to do one thing which seems irrational, perhaps even unpleasant, in isolation. We can only know what they tell us at that time. It is not ours to know the greater picture which they oversee. If we could, then the mystery and challenge of existence would be obliterated, nothing learned and incarnation rendered useless. Also, as the bigger picture is always changing and evolving due to the actions and decisions (informed or no) of others, it would be pointless us getting a glimpse of it at one instant in time. As our Guides can see the webs that interlink us all more clearly from their overview they can give us advice on the best manoeuvre to make at that particular time. Given the threads of possibilities and probabilities that surround us our Guides can advise on which paths to follow.

Some events in our lives may be inevitable, fated and un-avoidable, whilst others allow us greater freedom of choice to make a different move than the one we were going to. The vast importance of being in contact with one's spiritual Guides, Guides that we all have without exception, is that they can show us the alternatives. They do this because they care, hence their allotted task of overseeing our incarnations. The nature, origins or forms of the spirit Guide/mentor will be more deeply addressed later but for now it is enough to state that their guidance is essential. Our guidance is a gift for us alone and so it is at very least a courtesy to consider our life moves with reference to what we are told.

Sometimes the guidance that we are given seems to be ridiculous at best and horrendous at worst. Sometimes when a person is certain that they have got it all sussed out and the future is clear to them then...dreams come, meditations reveal unexpected scenes and the Guides start saying some peculiar things! Let me lead you through a rather painful set of events that happened to me over the past year or so to bring you closer to my meaning. These events were unexpected to say the least.

They begin when I met Martin, as I shall refer to him. Martin was a man who I recognised instantly from past-lives which had been of ultimate importance to me. My first words to this man, a total stranger in this life, were "I know you!" So profound was my recognition of his soul that I dispensed with social nicety and said what I thought. I initially recognised Martin as a love of mine from centuries earlier. He and I had lived in Ireland, he had been a traveller and I had been married to a violent, drunken landowner. Martin bore such a striking physical resemblance to this old incarnation that I recognised him immediately in a physical sense. (Obviously our souls would have connected even if he had looked entirely dissimilar to the previous form he had worn in Ireland. The much-used quote of 'eyes being the windows of the soul' is so true. I myself have had many spontaneous memories of other lives come flooding back when I have locked eyes with a familiar soul in a stranger's body.) In the life I recognised Martin from, he, as my lover, had been brutally murdered by my then-husband. I myself had died after his murder. Our clandestine relationship had been the only thing that had kept me going, my marriage having been one based on violence and control. I had no reason to carry on living after the murder. I had remembered this life in Ireland when I had re-encountered the figure of the 'Irish husband' in this incarnation. The 'husband' was, unfortunately, as boorish and reactionary as he had been centuries before. He shared none of my past-life recall and had no knowledge of having met me before in Ireland. My own memories of other lives come back to me like memories from this life, with all the emotional pull of anything that has ever happened to me, no matter how different the circumstances of my life today. My soul is adept as throwing up these images and information to me because I have utter belief and assurance in the creed of reincarnation and so I let the memories flow through freely and with enthusiasm. I had never met another soul who felt this complete acceptance of their own far-memories. Consequently I had never received verification from anyone that they had been in the same place as me in another time. This was until I met Martin.

Martin knew exactly what I was talking about and even recognised the modern-day figure of the 'Irish husband', the man who had killed him in another life. It seemed at one stage that the scenario between Martin and the 'husband' may be destined to repeat itself but the 'husband' figure chose to do things right this time round and he simply wished

Martin and I well and walked away. I do believe that the 'husband' had needed to meet both Martin and I again in order to have the opportunity to make amends as his soul carried the burden of a murder. Although he was entirely unconscious of this need, the 'husband's' soul knew that it wanted to put things right and so it had desired us to all meet again. Bearing in mind the logistics in engineering three separate souls to meet again we can observe the power of the need of the 'husband's' soul. This, combined with my soul's need and Martin's soul's need made it fairly inevitable that our paths would cross again.

When one truly thinks about this sample scenario it is an awesome thing to comprehend how much web-weaving and energy shifting goes into such a fated meeting of three diverse souls. Each soul has many other souls that it needs to learn from or interact with. Clearly with a past incident as powerful as a murder the soul-link there was stronger than most. The urge for the souls to meet again and sort out their differences would also be stronger than most urges which drive us to encounter familiar souls again. Even if the manifest person is oblivious to the urge, the soul has its own agenda and will direct the personality it currently 'wears' to act accordingly. This follows the idea of the soul as eternal spark wearing a variety of masks when it becomes incarnate. It is the soul, not the current incarnate guise, which is the motivator. Although our current 'personas' have free-will, the urges of the soul are always felt. In the case of the 'Irish husband', his urges were deeply hidden in his consciousness. I am more aware of my own urges, being more connected to my own spiritual (soul) needs. My soul had an urge to meet Martin again through a motivation of overwhelming love. It was this love, not my need to 'seek revenge against my murdering husband' which drew my eternal soul back into this arena.

The connection between myself and Martin was instant and our need to be united in this life was unstoppable. Not only could he too remembered our Irish life and its terrible parting, but he also shared memories of other lives with me. Most notably was a dreadful incarnation which I would refer to as my 'key' incarnation. It was the life of a midwife-healer Wisewoman in fourteenth century France which ended with my rape, physical degradation and burning at the stake in a square in Avignon. Martin had been my only true friend and my spiritual love, a man named Julien de St Pierre, who came to visit me when I lived my peaceful existence in a humble one-roomed dwelling near Lyon. He and I would meet in the woods and our powerful passion for each other was purely of spirit as we never consummated the relationship. The full account of this moving story is given in 'Season of Sorcery', my first book which was published by Capall Bann in 1998. It is enough to state here that Julien tried to help me escape my inevitable persecution, only to end up ,by some cruel twist of fate, being captured and burned to death alongside me.

Such an intense spiritual connection followed by the memory of being murdered next to each other, helpless to do anything, was enough to bond our injured souls together across the centuries. I had screamed out to Julien as we died but he did not acknowledge me. This was due to his shame for not having saved me. The outcome of this soul-trauma was that we were bound to find each other again, to heal each other and to love each other as we never had in that life.

Our next coming together had been in that Irish incarnation, centuries later. Our souls must have been so tormented and traumatised by their last meeting that again our lives were blighted and our relationship was abruptly and violently severed. We had further incarnations in tandem subsequently, but they were set in innocuous circumstances whereby we may be together but not linked by love lest we be torn apart brutally again. Our injured souls could not have risked the damage of another tormented parting. It is fascinating to observe how our souls have engineered these roles, these

25

parts for us to play out in order for us to best learn and grow whilst recuperating from the shock of untimely and unpleasant partings and deaths.

In our current manifest roles we met again in this life. I instantly knew Martin and so all those huge feelings of love and pain returned. He also knew me, remembered our lives and could fill in any spaces in our story. He had his own spontaneous memories which had surfaced independently to mine. As he was eleven years my senior, most had occurred a long while before I had been mature enough to connect with my own. As we had lived at opposite ends of the country , there was little chance that we could have met or conferred in any way previously. Yet Martin had relived his life as Julien de St Pierre so completely, years previously, as to have physically manifested burns and wounds from the stake onto his flesh. He was certainly who I perceived him to be and I was also the woman he remembered from his lives. With such an overwhelming cosmic and karmic reunion what could possibly affect us? How could such a beautiful and destined relationship go wrong?

Before we had met, I had seen Martin in my meditations. He had seen me in dreams and on his astral travels. He had heard me cry out to him 'in spirit' and he even knew my name. We had searched for each other throughout this incarnation and had sent out our own spirits to find each other in meditations. (This 'finding' is astral-calling, a useful and successful psychic method of reaching other souls. I shall refer to this later with other examples of how it may be used for the good.) Martin could simply verify all that I had remembered, felt and seen before I had met him. He had experienced his side of these recollections and visions. It was an extraordinarily powerful link that we had and one that I was overjoyed with. Although I had total faith in my far-memory and visions it was still pleasing to gain another human being's confirmation of their validity. With the overwhelming bond we had in a spiritual sense we were still as open as anyone else to the wills and wishes of other souls, other manifest scenarios that had already been set up.Our connection and the profound inevitability of our union was marred by Martin's already being in a marriage, with a child.

As I am childless and have never married I was not as understanding as I could have been about the subsequent divorce and the dividing of the marital home. I was especially uncomprehending of the difficult and sensitive nature of the effect on him and the child at being separated. Although he had been an excellent father, inevitably the mother retained custody. Initially, I was accepting of everything...the child by another woman, the woman herself as a possible friend, the fact that Martin would have most of his possessions and money left behind tied up with the home and child....I was accepting because my spiritual guidance said categorically that we, Martin and myself, would have a child together, our own boy who would be called Michael Gabriel. In having this child we would 'enter the cornfield' as my guidance, and his, individually put it to us. By our fruitful union, the flow of energy would be good and we would finally have a peaceful, loving and happy incarnation on earth together.

Martin himself had been told this information by his own Guides, again and again. Before we even consummated our 're-union' we both knew independently of how our coming together was linked to the birth of this soul. I was told that it was the spirit of my Aunt who had just passed over and who dearly wanted to be born again through me. Her soul, recently gone on to the Other Realms, had overseen the coming together of myself and Martin. We had met at an event that neither of us had wished to attend which was not local to either of us. Martin was categorically told by his Guides (who he spoke to constantly) that he must go, as he would meet the woman he had seen in his meditations. His Guides stated that it was fated that we should meet. As he was going to the event with his wife he found this most unlikely, but went along with his trusted spirit Guide and braved the event. Martin and his wife were a partnership but not a love-match and their being together was based on the well-being of their child. Martin's wife had knowledge of her own soul-love and was keen to go to him (she herself is a noted psychic and writer who I shall refer to in another chapter.)

I myself had not wanted to go to the event, it was to be busy and noisy and I had to go alone as I had no one to go with. This was at a low point in my life and all I had was my spiritual Guide to go by. The choice was made that I should go. I vowed that if it were a lonely and unsuccessful day that I would never listen to my Guide again, but I was assured that there would be purpose and the man who I had sought for many years would be present. So he was!

The next period of time was spent with Martin and myself re-adjusting into our life together. This also meant our coming to terms with the disollution of Martin's marriage. Our conn-ection was so strong that everybody, including a very under-standing son, agreed we should 'go for it'. Our whole relation-ship was bound up around our guidance. Guidance stated clearly that we had to have this child. It was a union of two of the same, 'people of the greening' as we were called by our Guides. I had never wanted children and Martin at forty years of age was not considering another, yet we both implicitly trusted our guidance. We were given a path that we should follow in order for certain beneficial events to happen. However, as part of this plan for our new life, the Guides desired me to take on Martin's son and for us to move back into his house, whilst the ex-wife went to her lover. Had I have trusted, I can see how the pattern would have been so different. Had I have gone with the flow my trusted Guide suggested, Martin and I would be still together, soul-mates in harmony with themselves and others, with a boy-child and an older son. Thanks to me deciding to paddle against the flow, out of hurt, jealousy and fear, we ended up apart, with much damage done to all concerned.

I decided that I would not have this child. Having initially welcomed the romantic notion of giving birth to Martin's baby I then panicked and refused to go through with it. The reasons were based on a mixture of past-life fear and present-incarnation worries (I shall discuss the latter at length later in the book). Obviously I need not have had either as there was my chance, blessed by the Otherworlds, to overcome old patterns and phobias. Still I held on to the idea that I only had incarnations in which I was a spiritual recluse or some other single person in retreat from the world. I did not enter into family-based, child-centred lives. As a midwife in fourteenth century France I had lost a mother and baby which did not fill me with confidence about pregnancy or labour. The whole idea seemed alien to my soul which had repeatedly shied away from child-bearing scenarios. I knew that I was being given the opportunity to experience motherhood and the creative, feminine aspect in a loving and supportive environment with Martin. Yet I was still afraid. I just didn't 'do' pregnancy...it wasn't my thing! The Otherworlds were offering me a chance to get over these worries and to experience the singularly most amazing, powerful thing an incarnate body can do. I turned that opportunity down. Along with this opportunity, I broke a promise I had made to the spirits on my meeting Martin. I had broken the agreement I made to have his child. At that point...the energies changed. I changed them.

Also I did not wish to take on Martin's son because of the adolescent male energies he would bring and how they in turn would make me feel. These feelings came from my latent fear of male sexual energy as well as my opinions about the behaviours of modern men. Because of these fears and concerns I behaved very shabbily towards Martin's son who in reality was just a young man hurt by his Father's departure and not a threat at all. Admittedly, I was acting out of jealousy and insecurity too as the son was a clear reminder that Martin had been with another woman before me and had chosen to marry her.

I could understand where these worries came from, my having had numerous past lives featuring men who abused me because of my sex. I could also see that I saw Martin as my saviour, a man who was 'different'. Yet I was afraid to tackle these deep seated fears and I chose to carry on blocking them. I did everything else that was asked of me by my Guide but I steadfastly refused to acknowledge the ideas that I didn't like. I refused to have both my own child or to take on Martin's. I hid in Martin's love and hoped those issues would go away.

Inevitably our happiness was marred by this discord as well as other aspects like our terrible shared memories. We had so much to discuss and great pain to understand, combined with the fresh wounds of Martin's increasingly unpleasant divorce and the loss of his son. As Martin, in his Julien form, had not acknowledged me as we both perished at the stake, I had a deep-seated anxiety that he did not love me enough and that he would abandon me. Rather than discussing this fear, almost a terror, I pushed and pulled Martin emotionally to see if I could test his love. I refused to have his son around me, fearing he would love him more and leave me to be with him. I resented the son as a symbol of Martin having had another relationship before our all-consuming one.

I understand now that tapping into my poor, abused Wise-woman incarnation had left me with some fairly unstable mental and emotional links which I let fly at Martin. Although he knew what I was doing as he still listened to his Guides who told him the bigger picture, he also began to say 'no'. He would not have this child with me.

When we both refused the incoming soul which had brought us together astrally for the ultimate purpose of its rebirth, things began to fall apart. Manifestly we still adored each other, clung to each other in a world we both found difficult. Being part of a couple who had been terminated so cruelly opened up many old soul-scars about our fear and loathing of society as a whole. We retreated into our own world, holding on to each other as if drowning. Many other wounds opened up in us that had stayed closed previously. The energies were open, closed doors blew apart. We could not be so emotionally ebullient in one area and yet seal other parts away. We both were awash in a morass of past hurts and we would not let anyone else in to help us, Who could we trust? Sometimes we felt as if we were back in the woods of France together, the boundaries of time slipped and we could not distinguish incarnations and circumstances clearly. Old friends abandoned Martin in the bitterness of divorce and the rift between himself and his son grew due to his split loyalty between him and me.

In all this we could have found our level ground, we could have seen the bigger picture. But the Guides withdrew. We received only patchy advice and we could no longer see the bigger picture. I had gone against the flow and refused both his son and my son. In doing this, in going against something I had previously agreed to in order to have Martin, I had changed the patterns and the energies totally. The effects of such a decision were very far-reaching, whole realities had to shift to accommodate this change. Certain possibilities and probabilities were no longer open. Martin and I had been part of a web with strands which stretched off in all directions. I effectively severed the strands, leaving only one outcome.

Martin was devastated that he could no longer get clear guidance. All of his life he had received messages loud and clear, as had I to varying degrees. The constant love and support of his Guide was no longer a counterpoint to his life.

31

As an intensely spiritual man, one who had always flowed with the energies, he found this infinitely depressing. We started to visit outside clairvoyants for help, an activity neither of us favoured although we were desperate. The issue was, where should we live when we received Martin's meagre divorce settlement. The words came in loud and clear from the medium we consulted. I was not mentioned, although I sat beside her. Martin would live near water, he would do well and be happy. This worried us all the more, what of me ? This then made Martin worry that I would leave him. Emotionally battered, he began to withdraw from me, which fed my own anxiety. When we had been told by our Guides independently, repeatedly, that we would have happy lives this time, together, we felt cheated and hurt. Our Guides must be liars surely? We could not even agree on where we should live and we certainly were not going to come by the lovely cottage our Guides had promised us both in meditations. If our own Guides lied, we felt even more fragmented and alone, there was no basis to life at all, no spiritual core. We were emotionally exhausted and spiritually adrift.

One of the pieces of early guidance suggested we should not turn the dark haired child away if they asked for help. When Martin's dark-haired son asked to come and live with us I refused, in the face of the spiritual advice I had accepted before. This was really the final straw. I knew that what I was doing was wrong but I could no longer see any point in doing anything that I didn't want to do. I did not want Martin's son with me as a constant reminder of another woman. Martin no longer wanted my child, why should I have someone else's? What reward would there be in accepting an emotionally damaged adolescent into our home? When I refused this help and insisted Martin saw the boy outside of the home, things really disintegrated.

One may think that they would have fallen to pieces anyway, what with my attitude to the son, but this is not the case.

Martin and I had a bond which transcended almost anything, other people mattered but inside our tight circle there was nothing but each other. What did matter, ultimately, was our rejection of the process which had brought us together again and which formed a pattern which would have had benefits to many others. Not only the baby we were to have had, but to the son, the wife, the families involved, the friends and also to those we were supposed to have helped. Martin and I were to have had his old family home as a spiritual centre for healing and for counselling others. We were told in guidance that our relationship was so strong and our combined energies so harmonious and powerful that we could assist many others who would come to our door for help in the future. That door, that future, they never could exist once I turned my back on one part of the pattern. I had said yes in order to get Martin but as soon as it suited me I said no to the children. Therefore the line faded out that would have been, a possible became a void. It was only a matter of time before Martin and I followed suit. I knew this. I am certain someone as astute as Martin knew the reason for our untimely and excruciatingly painful demise.

We did not cease to be a partnership because of Martin's choice of home for us although I did not care for his choice. He decided on buying a narrowboat which was entirely un-practical for my creative lifestyle. Whereas once every decision was discussed, Martin bought the boat with an attitude that I could either live on it, or not, whichever I wanted. As life without him still seemed inconceivable I chose to go with him to the boat, as much as I disliked it. One night as I walked around the canal path where we had moored up I literally begged my Guide to speak to me again and to tell me plainly why Martin and I were not as we had been. I stood in the cold night air alone and I asked of them and they told me. They made me look up at the stars, look at the threads and the infinite links between all life and they made me trace the threads back. There I found the answer. I had rejected two souls who needed us. I had done this and all else followed. Was it repairable, this damage, I asked? The terrible truth was that it was not. I had effectively cut the line that was the core of Martin and myself. The link could not be mended. I had a choice and I had not chosen as advised. Now consequently I must learn. The extraordinary pain I felt at knowing that I had ignored something which could have been so loving, so strong and beneficial, was worse I am certain than any burning alive.

I did not cry for the lost chance right then, but I looked into a future without my soul- mate who I had spent much of this life longing for. That was one of the worst moments in my life, but I accepted it. I took the blame although my Guide did not accuse me. I asked him and I really understood and believed his answer. I knew that he was correct and I wished desperately that I had taken his other words as correct and as the truth. Guides do not speak selectively, one cannot disregard the difficulty or uncomfortable. Only they see the bigger picture and nothing we can do will be the wrong thing. What I did was not wrong, it simply wasn't the best course of action. But it had it's own lessons and new patterns and new possibilities, links and bonds sprang up to fill the void of a chance not taken.

For a while, the web was a tangle, chaos reigned in that quarter. New threads did form and something was forged from the emptiness. Emptiness my decision had created.

What of Martin and I? We could blame the choice, his choice, of the narrowboat as home. It did not suit me as an artist and writer, it was inevitable that I would leave its confines for a more suitable space. It was his boat and my home if I chose to stay but it was what he wanted. We no longer had a 'we' a couple decision, a partnership. He thought I would leave and I thought he was driving me out. The real truth to the end lay in the cold stars and the clear voice of my Guide. Neither of us ever vocalised this, although we wept alone about the lost life we were promised. Like a picture I had drawn from the visions of my meditations, it had been erased. I had the power, we had it, to erase a possibility. I had always seen the act of erasing an artwork I had created as extraordinary, I could make it exist, or not. So it was with Martin and I. He had been told, by other clairvoyants, that he would be on a tow-path of a canal. He had been told about him being with 'a woman of flowers' (Poppy?) and then 'another spiritual woman'. We had dismissed this too, although it too was true. I did not feature in his future, as seen by others.

We then both began to get fresh, clear guidance. I believe this is due to the shift of the pattern, the new possibilities forming astrally . Suddenly there were new choices, new events on the horizon. For me, Martin 'saw' a new relationship with a certain man who he described and later named. I dismissed this as he rejected any idea he would be with another woman. It was impossible. No matter how horrible our lives had become, we were still together and soul-mates could not part. How could we be with other people when we had been together as soul partners...it was unthinkable! No one else could compare to Martin, I thought, he was my ultimate. Yet the relationship became worse and worse.

I began to 'see' Martin in my meditations and the images were of another of his many incarnations. I did not feature in the life I saw him in. He was aware of this life as he had his own recall of it. Other clairvoyants had also mentioned it to him and it was obviously the next relevant incarnation for him to fully remember, explore and deal with. An incarnation without me.

If this was his next memory of a past-life to work through then why was it one we had spent apart? What did it mean?
I did the only thing I could do to act with as much (belated) wisdom and integrity as I could muster. I left the narrowboat.

35

I went back to Bath, where I purchased a caravan big enough to be an art studio and a make-shift home. I also found a part-time job working with profoundly disabled people. This seemed to me to be a penance, where I could positively help others far less fortunate than I.

I had said to Martin that I could not operate as a creative soul in the confined space of his boat but the reality was more complex than that. I knew I had to leave so that the next part of the process could take shape, I had done enough damage and by staying I was only holding up the inevitable. Martin obviously had spiritual quests of his own to tackle and therefore there must be something for me to do also. The fates and webs do not leave a void for long and I realised that I too would have a new purpose and destiny. I did not leave Martin with a light step. It was the singularly most painful and awful thing that has ever occurred, worse even than the moments at the stake in 1326 when Julien had not acknowledged me. Worse because this time I was choosing to leave my soul's-love because I knew that I had made a terrible, irreversible mistake and I could never go back. Done was done but the grief and emotional agony this move made me feel still resonates as I write. To leave one's love, not because you do not love him but because you know you have effectively term-inated any possibility of success in the future is a dreadful thing.

The futility of going over and over the events that led up to the dissolution is obvious but I myself am repeatedly drawn back to the blissful days of our reunion before I made the wrong choices. How could I not look back and consider where I would be today had I followed guidance? To know, via the spiritual advice of the Otherworld, what went wrong is very hard. I cannot pass blame on nor can I re-invent the past to be more palatable to me. I see the situation clearly now, with my Guide's overview. To walk away from someone that you still adore more than any other living soul, someone you have more in common with that any other, someone who is bonded to you across centuries....to do this is to know pain. What can come of it ,what purpose could such torment possibly serve?

Alone and clinging to the raft of my beliefs I began a new journey into the unknown. I would have been incredulous if a year previously anyone would have told me, Guide or no, that within two years of our union Martin and I would be living apart, less than ten miles from each other. That was the reality...he and I in our separate beds in our meagre accommodations trying to make sense and go forwards amidst the fresh grief of our demise. Martin refused to see me once I had departed his boat. It was too painful for him for me to leave and go home to a home that was not ours and vice versa, although I would have braved it just to spend time with him. He was right, even though I still was pulled to visit him on his boat (only to be sent back to Bath by him). Ours was a dead relationship, the future of which had been scrubbed out, terminated.

The residue of passionate love was something we both had to deal with in our own ways. Alone. I had to let go and go with the new flow. I had to accept all guidance I was getting, having learned that however unpalatable or hard the guidance is it cannot be selectively followed. New guidance stated that I had to let Martin go in mind, body and spirit. I should bury the bones of that relationship, grieve and walk onwards. Away from Martin.

Once I truly stepped away from Martin physically and spent time trying to gain spiritual clarity during meditations I began to 'see' again. Not only did I see that he would meet someone in the next few months (and that she would be connected with his past life that had been coming back to him) but that I too would meet someone as he had predicted. This seemed highly unlikely for the pair of us. Martin was as much of a loner as I. We had only been able to truly feel at ease with each other. We had been inseparable yet had found other company difficult. Neither of us were social creatures. I rarely went anywhere except to visit old established friends, usually female. Martin and I had always lacked the money or inclination to go and 'make friends', having too much of our own to deal with. However, guidance stated clearly that he and I were to be paired up again soon.

As I did not wish to be selective about the guidance I received I felt bound to ponder it. The thought of being with anyone, but anyone after Martin, who I considered to be the most compatible, most suitable partner for me, was ludicrous. How could anyone follow Martin? I felt miserable that I was destined to have some second rate relationship for some reason, how pointless! Unless it was more of a punishment? At this stage I still considered what I had done with Martin as being 'bad' and I felt as if I should have a thoroughly unpleasant time consequently. However, the universe does not operate thus.

Astrally and in the Otherworlds the patterns were shifting so as to accommodate new futures. The spirit of my Aunt which had been promised a new incarnation with Martin and myself was still active in finding me another partner. My Aunt's spirit was busy weaving a new set of circumstances in order for me to meet the appropriate man. Through my meditations which had regained their previous clarity I was told of my Aunt's endeavours. Meanwhile, another spirit of a man recently passed over to the Other Realms was busy weaving also. His endeavours related to the best possible outcome for his son. These were the energies at work as I began to receive clear guidance in meditation once again.

I had, before I had met Martin, had a long series of medit-ations about a Native American Indian. As my Guide is of this persuasion, or at least, he appears in form to be compatible with those energies, I was not surprised to see another Indian in my meditations. In these visions my Guide would show me this other man, a large silent figure on a horse. The Guide would place me on the horse with this other man and we would ride off into the woods. There would be a ceremony there of jumping a fire and later we would go off alone and make love. I remember thinking "but he's not my type at all!" whilst being surprised at our physical compatibility. These visions were very vivid indeed. I did not share them with Martin as they clearly had no connection to him and they had been prior to his arrival. In fact I only began having them again after his departure from my life. Not only this but I saw in my meditations that this union with the Indian had brought about a child, a boy. I saw myself nursing the baby and I was aware that in this guise my name was Running Deer. Myself and this tall, silent partner lived in a strange region of pines and snow but we seemed to be nomadic as I also recall arid desert type environments. I do know that our child died whilst we were in the cold snowy place and that my partner was devastated. I realised that my meditations were based on more than just fantasy or symbolic guidance. I was being shown another past-life memory. I realised this when I began to feel the very personal sense of loss at my child's passing and also the very real love I felt for my partner, the Indian.

I felt my having had a child was very unusual as I knew that I had never given birth in any other incarnation. One of the many myriad reasons as to why Martin and I should have had a child was that I had to learn not to be afraid of childbirth and children again. I had a fear of childbirth stemming back to my midwife life, losing both mother and baby during the delivery as I had done. Also previously in an even earlier incarnation I was a tribal healer, a man, and then I lost a child through ineptitude in my medical administrations. In this life I have a fear and loathing of pregnancy and giving birth which goes beyond my social worries about the whole procedure. I could never watch the films shown at school as part of sex education which involved birth. Similarly, at teacher training college I was supposed to watch a film depicting the birth process. I found they left me feeling so nauseous and afraid that I had had to leave the room. My having had a child in another life was rather astonishing and alien to me. I felt this incarnation had been a long while ago and obviously as a soul incarnating as female I had not experienced this 'female thing' since. In fact my lives had positively rejected partnerships and even in this life I was a natural loner and one who was not attracted to family life in the least. Still, the images came up in meditation, this man and the baby. I wondered where it would lead but tried to flow with it without fear or restraint. Why remember that life? It had to have a relevance.

Accompanying these meditation images of the Native Americans were two other incidentals. One set of images belonged to yet another life, in medieval England. These too I had remembered before I had met Martin. They were part of a complex story of myself as a young woman and a nobleman, Robert John, probably a Norman. He was my lover, a fine horseman and a powerful local influence. I myself was the feisty daughter of a more wealthy and titled man and I was bored of being the good woman at home. Here there were some lovely memories of my actually having a physical passion, something sadly lacking in my incarnations. This was a playful relationship with an element of danger and romance to it and it felt very pleasant indeed. However, it was terminated when my lover was injured in a tournament in front of me. This was most disturbing as I could not reveal my connection to him in public so I could not go to him. Robert John was later killed by a man in my Father's employ after a mutual acquaintance had told my Father of our affair at Robert's house. I have an intuition that I may have been pregnant then also, but memory does not stretch any further ahead than Robert's death. I think afterwards I was possibly sent away and locked up in a vast, forbidding building in the middle of nowhere as I recall gazing pitifully out at the world from a tiny window in a curved stone room. That is where memory ends. However, the relevance of the appearance of yet another far-memory involving a physical lover and a possible child is important at this point. I shall return to these memories as to their part in the scenario at a later point.

The fact that these memories arose spontaneously out of my subconscious again, when they had been obscured by Martin-related memory for nearly two years, was intriguing. Obviously the energies and patterns were shifting so rapidly that these memories resurfaced as part of the process I was as yet unaware of. It seemed at little soon for such things to be happening as I was still 'mourning' for Martin, but as they had been there in my meditations before he had come along they did seem familiar. I could only wait for what was coming.

As well as imagery I was visited by a spirit. He was nobody I knew and at first he said very little, he was just there in my minds-eye. He was obviously a spirit and he told me he had passed on yet I did not see him as 'a ghost' as one would expect. He appeared in my third-eye or inner vision and I was aware of him as a presence. His purpose was unclear, but he was pleasant and unthreatening. The over all feeling he gave was that he was watching me, getting to know me.

Whilst this psychic activity continued, I began to look at ways I could rebuild my life. I did not want to but I had to. One of the things I could do would be to start singing again. I had always sung with musicians in bands and I decided to take out a local paper to apply to anyone suitable looking for a singer. Whilst I was doing this I glanced amongst the 'partner search' section, what would have been known in less correct times as 'lonely hearts'. I was genuinely looking for a band to sing with, so why I did this on this particular occasion I will never know. The last thing I wanted was to replace Martin. Yet the advert leapt out at me and I found myself getting pen

41

and paper to respond. I had no qualms about writing in response to such an advert, I had placed them myself from time to time. In our society I see few outlets for meeting partners unless one is blessed with a very wide circle of acquaintances or social activities and not many of us have the time or money that such a scenario would demand. I did not question the validity of using the service, my only qualm was why I was writing to a stranger when I was still in love with Martin? I have no idea what prompted me and I felt terribly uneasy about sending the letter.

I do not see why the fates should not bring people together though a newspaper advert any more than in a pub or sports club. The amazing twists that mean we are brought together with the most suitable person at a particular moment are considerable. Why be in a certain place at that time, why be looking at a certain thing at that moment? The odds against me finding a past-life love through a random newspaper advert seem remote! What lead me to see that one-off placement in that particular edition? When one thinks about how it is we come across the important people in our lives it is inevitable that the complexities of such fates should be pondered. Which twist of fate engineered your own union with a loved one? Tracing back the strands can be an enlightening experience. I personally felt as if I had to respond once I had chanced upon such an appropriate advert. I did not expect the quick reply it received.

The person that placed the advert was called Robert. This immediately felt right. When we met I recognised him from...somewhere! He seemed pleasantly familiar like some very comfortable old jumper that had taken on ones own personal shape and smell. We had never met in this life but again, like Martin before, I recognised him. It was not the thunderclap response of meeting Martin but there was an extraordinary response in me to him that I was not expecting in the wake of my devotion to Martin. He was, as in my vision of the American Indian, 'not my type' physically and yet I was incredibly physically drawn to him in a manner I have never felt before. It was quite amazing to me that such an advert could pluck from the cosmos yet another man I had previously known yet there he was!

It only took a few more meetings for me to realise that the man-spirit who had been 'checking me out' was Robert's deceased Dad, passed over some months earlier. Robert's Dad soon began to give me messages to give to his son. As I did not know Robert well in this life I found it hard to tell him these messages, although he accepted them easily. It turned out that although Robert was, to all intents and purposes, a bog-standard biker type who did a regular job and got drunk all weekend, he had many psychic experiences of his own. He told me this in all earnest. He had never been that fascinated by them and they were not the result of drink or drugs. Once Robert connected more with me his latent psychism came to the fore. He began to pick up on both the Native American life and the life of Robert John in the Middle Ages. He, like Martin before him, could fill in the gaps which I could not see. He accepted that he had been both the Native American Indian and Robert John the horseman. Not only did he accept but he remembered for himself. If I had a flash of vision whilst I was with him relating to one of these lives he would see it too. Once, I saw him as the Native American holding up our dead child and screaming, as an image. Robert looked at me and asked "Why do I hear myself screaming?" I found that we could pass images between us spontaneously and also with effort. Robert was adept at picking up telepathic messages and feelings both whilst sitting next to me and when away from me. He was incredibly naturally psychic but very unpretentious about it.

For a man who had lived previously like any average single male, a life based strictly on material pleasure and gain, this was amazing. It amazed me more so than Martin, who was by nature aesthetic and spiritual with a life's dedication to psychic questing. Robert's previous disinterest was evident and indeed he found his newly acquired skills unremarkable. This was frustrating as I was used to discussing all things spiritual endlessly as it was my main source of fascination and interest. Robert would sooner discuss his fleet of motor-bikes!

Despite our connection, which grew ever stronger, between myself and Robert's deceased Father I felt myself questioning guidance again. I rebelled, I couldn't understand why life had placed me with this ordinary man who wasn't a bit like Martin. No matter about the visions of past-lives we shared, no matter that Robert's Dad said we should be together (and that he had helped bring us together). No matter that he said I was chosen to look after his son. I wanted to be with Martin, my true mate, not some 'average Joe' who couldn't help me or understand me in a million incarnations. What was going on? What was the meaning of dragging me from my soul's-love to put me with this situation?

The minute I protested and pulled away from Robert then things took an immediate down turn. My job became increasingly impossible, dealing with people with 'challenging behaviour' became more of a penance than I could have ever anticipated. Martin, despite my pleading would not entertain me. He refused to see me and would not write to me to help me understand why this was happening. I felt terrible and responded in the manner I have responded for centuries when something disturbs me. I shut myself away. I shut Robert out and turned him away.

The night I did this I had a vision in meditation. It was as clear as any I have ever had and it showed me Martin and Robert. "Choose" said my Guide. I could not bear to send Martin, my perceived soul-mate, away. How could I? So I watched Robert in my mind's-eye turn his back and walk away. The next day the actual physical Robert refused to talk to me and basically told me to get lost, which is hardly surprising. It was only when he had been so brusque to me that I sat on my own and contemplated life without his cheery, balancing input. Yes, he was opposite to me in many ways. He was a lot more capable of dealing with 'mainstream' society, events and people. He was easily pleased, worried little and was hard working, bright and enthusiastic. Moreover he was also extremely caring and loving, a man who found it easy to express his feelings in terms of cuddles and hugs. I had enjoyed this aspect of his enormously, as well as his good humour. I realised that he did me good, he was part of my learning to Be. What could I be for him if he was helping me to be more relaxed and receptive? I had to go into meditation to discover the answer which came from both my Guide and his Father.

Firstly, Robert was the only soul that had successfully managed to have a child with me although unfortunately this had been thwarted by death. We had a harmonious energy between us for creating life, our differences creating a good balance. This was reason for he and I to reunite and be successfuL again, for the good of the soul waiting to be born and for our own growth. I knew Robert did not wish to have children either....it was not only me who found the idea unnerving if not plain abhorrent. So why had our souls struggled together in order to birth one other soul? Partly because I had previously promised my Aunt's spirit that I would do this. Partly also because Robert's soul, if not his actual manly incarnation, was deeply wounded by the death of his child with me (in my life as Running Deer). He would be healed by our present union and fruitfulness. Robert's Father had brought us together as he thought I could best heal and care for his son who was also badly wounded in this life by his Dad's passing. Although Robert denied having feelings connected to the idea of us having a child, giving life to a spirit, his subconscious, his deeper Self, yearned for it with someone he could trust. Our physical union was better than the connection between Martin and I. Our balance made for a more harmonic blend. This was another reason why Martin and I had terminated although we were given a chance. Robert and I, although not intense spiritual mates, were excellent physical partners who would care for each other marvellously on the manifest levels.

Although my soul still felt desolate at a life without my spiritual love I could now understand the patterns of Robert and I. I had to discuss this with the Other Realms in order to get any clear sight. Alone it just made no sense. I would never have been with Robert again had it not been for my meditation and Otherworld guidance which revealed to me greater patterns and a larger more profound relevance than I could have guessed at. In meditation I 'saw' Robert who was huddled alone under a blanket. I was standing with Martin a little way away. As I saw Robert the ground around us began to split and shake. I had the choice to stay on the level ground with Martin who stood impassive. I looked over at Robert and saw a crack open up in front of me. If I wanted to go to him, I had to choose, quickly. I jumped the widening chasm and saw Martin get further away as the chasm opened up behind me. I went to Robert and held him, in pain inside because I had to let Martin go but feeling as if this was the right thing to do. I was told by my Guide that if I went with Martin I would be on the wrong path and nothing could get me back. Yet now I was on the path I was meant to be on, following the advice of my trusted Guide. I didn't know where I was going but I had made the right choice this time. I trusted the flow and went with it, painful or no.

Robert accepted me back after I had jumped that astral ravine to choose him. I know it was the right thing, although I still do not fully comprehend why Martin now lives about fifteen miles away and I never see him. I do, however, trust that the universe is unfolding as it should be and that whatever happens, this is the right road for me. Perhaps I am fortunate to have felt the intense pain of such a connection, to have been truly awoken on all levels. But as mine and Martin's previous incarnations show, such incredible spirit-love does not work well on the Earth-level, a level not designed for such purely ethereal adoration and devotion. On this level we must interact with the world and with others who may not be so 'of our type' in order to learn and grow. Martin is undoubtedly of my type, but our closeness and our bond may have made our functioning in the reality of the World unfeasible. Perhaps he and I need to be with a balancing influence in order to learn from being incarnate? Perhaps then, he and I will reunite with our lessons once we pass over? Maybe it was enough that we have experienced the exquisite rightness of soul-connection, a feeling which cannot be sustained in this inhospitable social climate?

Martin made me want to cling to him, shelter in him, hide away, just us. I do not think this is a good or profitable way to live, it is self-serving and stunting no matter how it feeds the soul. We certainly do not incarnate to remain apart from the world, not matter how unpleasant that world may be. Security and safety are not necessarily the best places from which to become the soul we were fully meant to be. Lessons are not learned in hiding, from security. Out on the 'right' road now I am insecure, I experienced periods of panic and "what if...if only" yet I have to keep going because I know that one day, in this life or another, my part in the pattern will make sense.

Looking at your own life thus may reveal a greater clarity, searching for connections and meaning along paths that may have seemed the wrong ones to take at the time. In retrospect perhaps we can see a pattern as to why we subconsciously chose a direction that may have seemed irrational or strange at the instant of choosing. This is why it is futile and damaging to regret or look back in anger. With the overview that the Guides can give and with the distancing of time we may come to discover the threads of our lives, woven between us and the Otherworlds. By this I may understand that Martin and I may only have met to lead me to the place where I am today. One day, I will gain the bigger picture but for now I know I stand where I should be standing.

Perhaps Robert and I are not meant to be eternal partners but in our union we have chance to enrich and enhance each other and others through the energies we create. Energies not of retreat but of response and interaction. This may frighten me as I was used to utter security in Martin, but it challenges me, makes me consider my Self and why I have such fears and needs.

For Robert, I know his Father is satisfied with my nurturing of his beloved son. He has, according to what I have been told in guidance, moved on to another incarnation, his job of 'providing' for his son is over and done. I found it fascinating and reassuring to see photographs of Robert's Father, which I finally saw after the spirit of the man had departed to his new life. Robert's Father had always appeared to me in long shorts and a beret with a backdrop of a desert, incongrously with a sheep dog! When I saw a group photo of him in the army I recognised him immediately from the throng. He had appeared to me as he was happiest, a younger man in army clothes during his work in the Middle East. His trusty dog came from later in his farming life and had become his companion in spirit. I had already described to Robert the man who had been communicating to me as his Dad and so he was pleased to finally be able to show me the photographic evidence. Now I have seen his Dad I have no doubt that he was with us and was responsible in part for our coming together. This alone makes the transition worthwhile for me an affirmation that my spirit work is 'real'. The man in the photograph was certainly the man who had first visited me in spirit before Robert and I had met. I started this book with

48

this very personal example as I feel that it gets across an important message. Go with the flow! Know what the spiritual tides are and move with them. This is not easy as I have described. In my case it was far easier to rebel or fight the flow. The satisfaction that such an action achieves can only be temporary. There was a certain way that was the best way and if those energies are blocked then that possibility terminates. The chaos we create by doing this will soon settle into new patterns...this is natures way...only the new pattern will not be that original way that was offered to us, that which was most harmonious to our true selves and to the All.

The best possible outcome is offered to us as part of the flow. If we know this and deliberately reject it (as I did out of fear, anger, insecurity etc.) then we must accept the consequences. The best possible outcome may appear strange, the guidance may seem bizarre and the path offered not desirable. To go with the flow is to go with it knowing that one day it will all become clear as to why we were lead that way. Guides are not tricksters, we are not guided a particular way for the hell of it! This is why it is vital, as a psychic or spiritual practitioner, to have that close working relationship with a trusted known Guide (but more on this later).

The beauty of the spirit mentor or Otherworld Guide is that they give us a glimpse of the great cosmic web that connects us all. We have access to past, present and future via the Guide. Through our meditation and our spirit links we may be given the opportunity to flow with the most appropriate energies. As always, we have free will. My experience tells me that we may choose to say 'no'. That is not, as I have shown, the wisest thing to do.

Not only do we benefit personally from acknowledging and moving with the energies but it also affords us the insights to treat others more appropriately. As we can 'see' more clearly as regards life and our interaction with all life, so we may gain greater understanding of the nature and energies of others. We need no longer see people as one-dimensional and need not take the situation at face-value. We may, through a little effort in meditation, gain much understanding about all parts of the energy matrix, not only our own. We can see the patterns and know that we all connect. We can be amazed at the subtle, complex, beautiful webs which bring us together and move us apart again. Over and over, with flow and harmony. We need only spend a little time in contemplation to hear truths which affect many lives, many incarnations. The information is there for us all if we listen and accept.

Going with the flow is not about denying our own needs as individuals. Nor is it about ignoring the needs of any other individual. It is about genuinely understanding that we are not temporary beings. Our existence as a soul, our influence, goes on and on. Souls do not end, they continue to grow, learn and Become in a variety of contexts. By this we may flow more easily, at ease with the truth that it may take us lifetimes to understand why we were best advised to do something that at that time seemed like the wrong way.

Chapter Two

Dreaming Harder

It is true to say that if I want something, I generally get it. The 'it' can range from a pair of shoes that I desire to the change of my circumstances including job, home and partner.

In the case of needing a particular new item of footwear it is simply a case of imagining that I already own it. I focus the item before I go to sleep and with this focusing comes the strict code of it harming none that I discover and buy this shoe. I then allow myself to be lead as to when I go out shopping and as to which shop I am lead into. This is one hundred percent effective. For clothes I genuinely need for a purpose I do the same and am even amazed myself at the speed in which I come across the exact garment in a second hand establishment. I have tried this for others with less success as I find it harder to put enough desire and will into the matter, yet I still achieve their wants eventually and as close to their idea as possible. The power of visualisation and will is undeniable. Wishing works. I can change things, by wish and will.

The most rapid 'turn-over' I achieved for finding something that I needed was a few hours! Whilst at work one afternoon I began thinking "I would love an old fashioned trunk, it would be so useful to keep such-and-such in". I filled in the dull hours before I could go home daydreaming up an elaborate fantasy as to this trunk and what I would use it for. Consequently, on my return home from the job some hours later I discovered an old metal trunk propped up outside the door to my flat! It was entirely empty and had no message attached.

It was not perfect and it needed a lot of cleaning and painting but it was exactly the size I had wished for. On taking it indoors I realised the sheer magnitude of my will and its extraordinary effects. My fertile imagination and my developed ability to visualise, combined with my determined focus and clarity could literally make things happen then same day!

If the webs of possibility and probability allowed for it there was an endless scope for what I could 'magic up'. Magic being the direction of will, in this case with all good intent and without needless coveting. I personally would never wish for things beyond my need or use and I could never justify using my own powers to gain practically pointless, ostentatious items. That would be an abuse of power that I would find ethically unacceptable, although clearly this is up to the individual.

I never did discover how the trunk got there, I can only assume that my wishing coincided somehow with someone wanting to ditch an unwanted item. As I lived on the top floor of a block of flats and this would have meant said (hypothetical) person dragging the thing up three flights of stairs, (somewhat out of their way) I found this scenario a little difficult to accept! There again, I could hardly picture the trunk materialising out of thin air on my doorstep either! Although it is not beyond the realms of possibility, probability suggests not. Still, I never did get an insight as to its appearance there.

Of course, dwelling on a new pair of boots or a trunk is nothing in comparison to the complex set of circumstances and interactions that would necessitate a life-change. How many people and patterns must I effect to bring about a relocation or career leap? Imagine the webs stretching out from you and how such life moves would radiate out from you in an endless pattern of cause and effect. Quite a feat to bring about a harmonious change of such magnitude! However, I have always managed to achieve these aims although they have seemed impossible or inconceivable to my conscious mind. My problems get 'wished out' eventually, depending on the complexity of the moves involved for all. Because of my close involvement with my Guide and the Otherworlds I am able to discover the best, most harmonious, path for me to follow for a desirable outcome. Therefore my life-wishes tend to blend and harmonise with the path that I see as being the more beneficial for all concerned. One can observe the message of what I am saying here by two examples.

Firstly, when I was alone and desperate to understand my own psychism and far-memory I wished for the man who had haunted my dreams to come back to me. I wanted him to 'save' me from the life I was leading. The man I wished for was Julien, someone who had tried to save me from execution as a Witch in the fourteenth century. It seemed highly unlikely to my rational self that I could find the reincarnation of this man alive and well in twentieth century England.

Meanwhile, unbeknownst to me the man who had been Julien was indeed incarnate and doing a spot of wishing of his own. In this life he was called Martin and he was doing a great deal of focussing on meeting me again as he too was unhappy. His marriage was blighted by his wife's love of another man and he saw a positive outcome in letting his wife go free so that he could meet me again. Of course, he did not know if I was alive or dead either, but his Guide gave him hope. Not only hope, Martin's Guide eventually gave him the exact place to find me (such is the blessing of having a good working relationship with one's Guide!) Martin and I put a lot of wish and will into our meeting again on an individual basis entirely unknown to each other at the time. However, there are always other variables of energy involved in any psychic 'transaction' even in a wish, or spell.

The change was only brought about so swiftly because of other circumstances reflecting out from our core need. I needed 'saving' very badly at that point in this incarnation as my despair about myself and my life was reaching near fatal proportions. My next step was inevitably suicide. My deceased Aunt had plans for me as to her own reincarnation and was not about to let me slip away from this mortal coil. This and the need of Martin's wife to be free to follow her path were contributing energies. Martin and I were united with the following equation of energies:-

Focussed visualisation (wish and will) by myself and Martin, Plus inner knowledge from our Guides of the most harmonious outcome. Plus desires and energies of others involved directly (Martin's wife and the spirit of my Aunt) equals a swift and balanced realisation of need which harms none.

By Martin's being close to his Guides and my ability to focus and 'see' we were led to an appropriate destination. Because the will of my Aunt and the wishes of Martin's wife added to the matrix we were even more firmly linked. Thus the union came about fairly swiftly. I have no doubt that my wishing, dreaming and visualising for this eventuality aided the process beyond measure. If I willed hard to find a pair of appropriate shoes then imagine how much more energy I put into finding my soul-love! I sent out an astral call for him just as I would astrally send out an S.O.S for the shoes to be donated to a charity shop at just the right moment for me to buy them.

Secondly, with the scenario with Robert, I was filled with a desperate need to leave the canal boat I shared with Martin at that time. My relationship with Martin was a shadow of its former self due mostly to our refusal to bear a child and to care for Martin's son.

Unbeknownst to me, Robert's own life was in turmoil with him recently losing his Father. This was compounded by his girlfriend of some years leaving Robert to be with his friend. This combined with his dead Father's will, to see his son happy and cared for and my Aunt's will to see me with a suitable mate was a potent blend.

My Aunt knew that she was being denied access to incarnation through my union with Martin and that she must find me a new match. As my psychic link with the Otherworlds was far more developed than it had ever been previously I was able to trust in my spiritual guidance more and my guidance told me that I should indeed leave the boat for the best possible outcome for all...including my Aunt. I knew this to be for the best even though it seemed half madness to give up on my soul-mate for some unknown future. Because I stepped into that unknown future with good faith then I was further guided with clarity and love to do still more unlikely things, which I duly did. These things included answering Robert's advertisement and then following up this unlikely relationship against the will to remain linked to Martin forever.

I had begun with the wish to leave in December and by April, due to my listening to my Guide, I had a new home, a new man and a new job. My focus on leaving the boat had been strong enough and it in itself was a catalyst to set the other energies and events in motion. However, I would say that other wills here involved were equally strong and had a greater part to play in the swiftness of the affair.

Had I spent time, in this instance, focusing on exactly the dwelling I wanted and where, it would have no doubt been a longer and more painful process. As I asked only for the most suitable dwelling for me at that time to help me leave the boat then my wish was granted sooner. I knew that I should go and so saw no need to delay the inevitable process any further.

This may sound cold and distant when in fact the move was agonising.

When one is truly in touch with the Guide and receives solid guidance then life often becomes harder and more painful, the way of the psychic is not glamourous and obvious rewards may be slow to show themselves. Because of my quick surrender and the intervention of other patterns of energy the meaning behind the transition became apparent quite rapidly.

Of course, with both examples there is also the subconscious will and wish of the soul that should be added to the equation. The soul has its own hidden agenda which we can access through mediation but which remains concealed from our rational, conscious self. In each case both my soul and the souls of Martin and Robert had wishes to meet again. Past life links can be positive and reciprocated...i.e two lovers wishing to be reunited in another incarnation as here. Or, as we will see in the following chapters, they can be one-sided needs and only one soul of a group may have the wish to replay a scenario in order to get it right. Therefore the wishes of former murderers, adulterers or thieves may have to be taken into consideration in certain equations. One soul may have no active wish to see another again, whilst the others need is so strong that they manipulate situations to fit their own requirements.

Here, however, the wishes of both souls were for a positive reunion as their previous attempts at relationships had been cut short or thwarted by circumstance. The equation of the (re) union of Robert and I reads as follows:-

My will and wish to leave the narrowboat and to make a new life, Plus my need to meet Robert (specifically) due to our past-life links (subconscious need) Plus Robert's need to find a new loving partner to help heal him, Plus Robert's need to meet me again due to past life links (subconscious need) Plus the desires of my Aunt and Robert's father to find us suitable loving partners Equals swift and fated change which benefits all concerned.

What of Martin in this equation...of his needs, will and wishes? Although our demise and my departure were excruciatingly painful for the pair of us (as our manifest conscious selves could not comprehend why we should have come to such an end) Martin's inner wisdom and soul knew that he too had a fate and destiny separate from mine. Neither of us could believe on an earth-level of relating that our soul-love should have come to nothing.

It seemed to render all other loves or futures pointless and without light and hope. Yet from both of our individual inner visions and meditations we both knew deep down in our very core of being that we both should be somewhere else. It was me that started the chain of energies for this move to be possible. I believe this was because it was me who first understood the futility of our relationship now we had closed the door on our promise to give life to a child together. I had to be the one to step out alone. It was hard, far harder than the mere words here could ever convey, but when one's Guide tells you to go then it is wise to follow. I had learned the hard way about the pitfalls of ignoring guidance.

In retrospect now I can see a bigger picture and I understand more of why I had to do what I did although the pain is still fresh and real. Imagine how much more the Guide sees and knows with his or her overview. This is why trust is imperative in them, and getting to know them is essential to forming this trust. In terms of an equation this reads:-

A good working relationship with one's spirit Guide. Plus accepting their words as coming from a wider perspective. Plus understanding that we may not comprehend the advice yet but ultimately we will (faith). Plus acting positively in the world on the above. Equals the most harmonious outcome - change.

What of understanding that knotty issue, that of why myself and my supposed soul-mate Martin did not 'make it' as a partnership? From where I am now I can be intensely grateful for my short time with Martin. I am profoundly touched by his love, wisdom and kindness. Perhaps it is now my duty to spread this love? A friend of mine commented wistfully that I had been blessed to have had experience of such a love as she herself had not even glimpsed. I thought at the time that this was romantic nonsense as how could I possibly be blessed whilst feeling such pain? As time passes I do see the point she was making for I am now opened to love and appreciate in totality the fragility of love in the world. I feel as if for a time I dwelled in the Otherworlds, in a place where there can be perfect peace and perfect love. it is because of this Other-worldly feeling that Martin and I cannot function as a unit in 'the world'.

Being so blissfully unaware of 'the world' and dwelling in our own heaven is not conducive to learning and in manifest form, incarnate, we are here to learn and to grow. Maybe we have to learn our lessons separately, without distraction, to bring them back to the soul-unit in death? Our brief time together may have been 'touching base'...a soul fortification and no more. Do similar souls gravitate towards each other in an inhospitable world for a rest together before moving on in the dance? I strive to understand the meaning of something that can leave someone feeling so entirely bereft afterwards. I also strive to comprehend the meaning of 'soul-mate' as someone who may help us grow and learn - our dynamic, comple-mentary opposite rather than our spiritual double.

Judy Hall, an author and therapist with many years exper-ience of past-life issues has valuable insights into the soul-mate question. She too puts forward the notion that a true soul-mate may be someone with whom we spark, with whom there are challenges, debates, differences. Perhaps they are those with whom we find a balance of energies not an exact reflection of our own. Judy suggests that many of us believe everything in the garden will be rosy when we meet 'the one'. Her challenging of this is that the soul-mate is the one with whom we go to hell and back as a learning process...not a punishment. Obviously, as Ms. Hall also agrees, there are those with whom we will find learning more harmonious and these may be a soul or souls from our own 'base group'...souls of our type. Perhaps, from my individual perspective, both Robert and Martin are from my soul group, different as they may seem from each other? If Ms.Hall is on the right track then it will be Robert who is the most beneficial soul-mate for me in incarnation...he being a complementary opposite to me, not a psychic double as Martin was.

If there is indeed only one true soul-love and Martin is mine then my time with Robert seems pointless and tragic. Yet I cannot feel that way. I cannot conceive of a relationship being worthless. Even if another soul intervened in the pattern and I was left without both Robert and Martin I would have no regrets. Even if Martin is my soul-love and even if my relationship with Robert is temporary then I must understand that all that has happened has been necessary to make me who I am and to put me where I am. I can be assured that I have taken the most harmonious steps even if I do not understand why. Judy Hall suggests that soul-mates may not be forever but for 'as long as it takes'.

What is the key to willing and wishing? To focus on the best possible outcome, to visualise for it, to energise it. Obviously by best possible outcome we mean its positive effect on people and the environment. Two things here...clearly we cannot know everyone that we effect as our actions have very far reaching consequences, always. I do not know how I influence a stranger's day when I say 'good morning' to them in the street. Perhaps my one cheery greeting would change their reaction to someone else that day, and so on. It is enough to wish for the outcome, not to know every inch of what may happen and to whom. Careful thought may be given to this in relation to immediate persons and no more, it wastes time and dissipates energy.

Also, the best possible outcome may seem like a pretty odd thing at first. It can take years, maybe even lifetimes, to appreciate why some unlikely event had to happen. The trick is to flow with the guidance and to trust in the known Guide. In this way we can have an appreciation of the web of life that brings us to the places we need to be. This may be with rapidity (in the case of my trunk) or over a period of time suitable for the 're-shuffle' required. It may answer your need in a strange or unexpected way but it will none the less answer it.

The need may be specific...a red boot, a ballet shoe....or it may be simply for a home of ones own. It is often wiser to request something which (if it harm none) is appropriate for the self at that time. When I wished for 'a home of my own' and ended up in a rickety old caravan then some may interpret that as wish failure! Going with my flow and listening to my guidance I knew that this rather inadequate home was necessary and that also it was temporary. In this case I told concerned friends not to worry about me in my damp and ramshackle caravan. I had been told by my Guide that I would be moved out by September if I let go and went with the energies. Sure enough, by September I had moved in with Robert and had gained my tattooing apprenticeship!

I did not let my pride about gaining such a poor type of home get in the way of the fates on that occasion. I had to learn flexibility and it would not have been beneficial my getting stuck in a more permanent abode. So what if the caravan leaked...I could focus on a dry summer, or at very least I could wish for a wind which blew any rain across the caravan roof rather than it pelting directly down on it! I haven't always been so good at making the best of things but it surely helps!

Another example is my career. In order to get out of teaching, a profession I loathed as it was in essence the complete antithesis of my nature, I wished vaguely and in a non-specific way to 'get out'. Indeed, my ill health achieved this aim and landed me in a situation where I was reliant on benefit and trapped in that circle of claiming which is hard to see a way out of. I had to wish and will entirely specifically to force myself out of the all-pervasive energies of the claimant...a lifestyle which appeals due to the freedom but conversely suffocates because of the control an outside body has over one's finances and doings. I myself could find no personal respect in claiming although I did find the time to be creative a seductive element. I wished for independence through a creative job which did not compromise 'me'. My focus was on such a means of earning enough to live on whilst utilising my unique talents for art and communication.

Although I left this fairly open, I had tattooing in mind. I did not wish too hard in case this idea was inappropriate. I left to fate the exact destination, but gave full attention to focussing on the needs this destination must fulfil. I wished for it. Within four months of my wish and focus I started my tattoo apprenticeship! This was against many odds yet the way opened up for me easily. I did not focus specifically on tattooing but it fitted the energies I had focussed on...it benefited me financially, creatively and as an individual.

As an example, when I took up the challenge of becoming a tattoo artist I had to consult with the Guide as to any potential effects I may have on my future clients. I did not know of these hypothetical clients but I had to check with the Guide if me taking on the responsibility of indelibly marking people was a positive thing. I do not think that the Guide can

'see' on and on into oblivion. Nor could the Guide tell me categorically that all the people that I ever tattoo would be
enhanced and not damaged. The Guide could give me an
overview of the general energies involved and how my being a
tattooist would affect those strangers I would immediately
come into contact with. It is prudent for me to keep checking
this from time to time to get an update on how my energies as
a skin artist affect those I work on. This can be translated
into any profession where one directly affects someone else's
life permanently. Saying this, no interaction is as permanent
as a tattoo. In this I am even more aware to treat the act of
tattooing as an intensely spiritual act which changes someone's energies forever.

Something that applies to any other job in which one works
closely with strangers/others is that I do not 'take on' the
client's pain or anxieties. As a 'psychic sponge' I am entirely
susceptible to picking up every bit of astral rubbish from my
clients. I used to leave each session exhausted and ill but now
have begun using my psychic 'green cross code' to protect
myself, a discipline that everyone who works so closely with
people would be wise to adopt. I am actually hands-on in
someone's aura so I am extremely careful.

When I was on the beginning of the path as a tattooist I was
faced with many difficult tasks, finding suitable premises and
such like. Judging by the speed and ease with which this was
achieved with I can only guess that I did well in my choice
and that my will was well directed. This career was brought
about by my singular focus on what I could do to earn money
in a creative way, most importantly in a way compatible with
my soul-type. I had been mistaken before in working against
my soul-type, as with teaching in yet another bid to flatten
myself to societies' shape and to be liked and accepted.
Teaching gave me a degree of respect and understanding from
society that I shall probably never have again yet it was not
'me'. Nor do I now crave this acceptance, all I ask is that I am

fulfilling my own potential and being who I be. As with everything here, the advice is to work with the energies and to do this one must learn to feel and see them. What would you consider to be the equation for the criteria to form a wish, bearing in mind all that we have to consider before formulating the wish itself?

To quote comedian Billy Connolly "everyone's born to do a certain thing and if you're dead jammy you find it...and if you're good at it keep doing it...until you're fed up and then find something else! You're here to make babies and look after the place...you know ?!" This puts a good perspective on what best to wish for!

I have total faith in the effectiveness of working with the energies that connect all life. Psychic work in this way is effective and fast acting. With the Guide and Otherworlds in one's sights then there is no 'wrong' way, only a most harmonious way that we can chose to work with, or not. There are lessons on taking any path, the lessons on the most advised path are those that we need at that time... the others will only lead us back there, eventually. The most harmonious path, as we have seen, can appear to be the least appealing. We will only ever recognise it by tuning in to the subtle messages of our own soul, the gentle advice of a loving Guide.

To conclude, I will give an example of how wish and will are strong magic. Magic which can easily last and linger long after we ourselves have forgotten about it. Magic which can affect others against their will.

My example comes from a daydream of mine, similar to the 'trunk' scenario, created to fill in a bit of time when I was bored at work. Only this time I focussed on a person, not an object. I imagined what they thought and did, where they went after work, their personal tastes etc. I saw this person at work all the time but never really got to know them due to time pressure or because others were in the way. Due to my boredom and because of my imagination I began to create fantasies about meeting this person after work and going for a coffee with them, only to discover they lead a fascinating social life... which of course they invited me into! I spent a lot of time staring at this person and imbuing them with all sorts of characteristics and attributes, just as I would with a character when writing a story, which I do often.

Eventually this person began to notice me and obviously became aware of my psychically dwelling upon them. They were uncomfortable around me without seeming to know why. I noticed they would stare at me perplexed or walk away, embarrassed if I came by. My 'innocent' daydreaming about them had begun to affect them unconsciously on a deep level, though they clearly had no idea what was going on. I continued to fictionalise and fantasise about this individual until I left that job.

At that time I realised I was a psychic but I had no idea what my focus could achieve. After leaving the job I subsequently met Martin and forgot all about my previous daydreaming, which after all had been harmless entertainment to my bored creative self...or so I thought. It wasn't until after Martin and I had finally split up and when I had a far greater understanding of my own psychic ability/power that the evidence of my 'daydream magic' showed itself. The person I had put so much focus into turned up at my door, unannounced, and declared he was in love with me. He appeared to be utterly clueless as to why he was doing what he was doing and he looked alarmingly glazed and confused...not his ordinary composed self at all.

All my 'meaningless' attention had affected his subconscious. I had bombarded him with so much focus that the only way he could interpret his feelings about it was to assume he was feeling some irrational love or attraction for me. In fact I had

just agitated his aura and jangled his etheric self so much
that he had to feel some connection to me as I had made a
powerful one to him. However, he was no more in love with
me than my daydream had ever been about the 'real' him.

What a thing to do to someone and what a lesson in the power
of the psychic Wildwitch when focussing intently! It is not
vanity to acknowledge the power...it is common sense!
Thankfully I had the sensitivity and understanding of the
subtler energies to disentangle us both from that situation
and to heal the damage I had caused in that person's energy
matrix. It is one thing to wish and focus on a trunk but quite
another matter to do so about another human being,
repeatedly and with intensity. Imagining is magical; I imagine
and I dream in full colour with sound, sensation and smell.
Imagining good things about one's lover is quite another
matter to invading someone else's space with expectations
and scenarios which are inappropriate. This is why I will
never perform a 'love magic' for anyone without both people's
consent. I have done that in the past and had to do a lot of
healing and repairing on that occasion also! Never underestimate the way you can effect the energies by visualisation.
Always check any focussing - a magical act - with the trusted
Guide first.

This brings me to unwanted psychic intervention. Unless
someone directly asks you to help, or if you offer and they
accept the help, then do not intervene. You will not be
thanked for this unethical move, no matter how well meaning
you are. All the Witch can do is to place the cares of others in
their astral 'safe place' and have it dealt with by others who
know more what they are doing, Guides and Avatars. To ask
for healing for the people and problems is fine, send them to
the place where they need to be for such healing to happen. To
undertake unrequited healing on one's own is tantamount to
snooping around the recipient's bedroom whilst they are out.

Is this too strong an analogy? An unasked for intrusion is an unrequired act. I have myself been reprimanded by friends for letting unrequired guidance slip out during my letter writing. I do not usually realise what I have done but the recipient of my letter can get quite peeved if they think I've been snooping around their astral body without their per-mission. Worse still they may believe I've been rummaging around in their thoughts as often the guidance that I let slip comes to as question they have not yet vocalised. No-one takes kindly to such intrusion. I did not mean to intrude. I connect with a loved friend in letter form and immediately I pick up snippets from them out of the ether. I tune in to their trans-mission, if you will. I have to guard against this which is an effort but at least stops friends being offended that I rudely spied on them astrally.

To dream harder we must invest time. It is a true to say that every thought is a prayer and should be used as such. A final equation on this subject and a code of practice would read:-

Identifying the real core need
Plus checking that this is appropriate with the Guide
Plus focussing on it in a clear psychic space,
Plus giving it 'dreamtime', energy and life,
Plus wishing for it to harm none,
Equals harmonious satisfaction of the need.
Equals successful magic! (without the need for robes, props and regalia...magic the wild, natural way!)

We must understand in our hearts that we are pure energy and that we radiate that energy outwards. This energy can be shaped. As manifest reflections of the divine spark we can play a part in the Dance of Life and Death, weaving the webs, observing the myriad strands of probability and possibility. We are responsible for change, we can effect change... but we cannot control. Part of our responsibility is to shape the energies with as much knowledge of the consequences as the

Guide may share. As Witches with the abilities to use such power then we must be careful, ethical, sensitive and courteous. There is no such thing as a free lunch and with all knowledge comes a weight of responsibility. Yet this need not make us too heavy to dance. Indeed, our steps on this Earth may become lighter, freer, knowing we act now with more love and more understanding. Knowing we can change, if it is our will.

Our energies are everything, everything is energies.

Again, another question to close this section. It is taken from 'The Greenwood Tarot' (Thorsons 1996) by Mark Ryan and Chesca Potter and it is a description of the card in the major arcana, the Fool. Perhaps this powerful, eternal archetype has the key. The description sums up so beautifully the essence of this section.

"The Fool stands on the white chalk cliff edge poised to step into the abyss. His face is calm and unworried and his gaze rests on the future with a slightly curious expression. He greets this leap into the void with open arms and trusts the wings of imagination and honesty to carry him over the gap to the lush green turf of a new path."

What does the Fool have that we should strive for?

Chapter Three
Walking with Spirit

The Guide, the spiritual mentor or Guardian Angel figure, is the singular most important figure in a Witch's life. Just as everyone born into the world has a belly button, so too do they have a Guide. That is, a spiritual figure who has chosen to track them for part, or all, of their life-journey. If the former is true then the Guide who begins the task will be succeeded by another more compatible to that portion of the persons life.

Guides do not come and go with the seasons but can change during the course of a life. Although we may receive guidance from many and varied sources during meditation or psychic work, the Guide is always the constant, one we can refer back to and check things with. Other spiritual presences may be drawn to us at certain times but they will not have the rock-solid bond and connection with us that the Guide has. The Guide does, after all, invest one hundred percent of his or her time in supporting us, watching us in a way that no-one else can...without judgement and with unconditional love.

The Guide is ultimately closer to us than any other being and has chosen us specially to devote their energies to. They are our sacred link between our realm and theirs, between life and after-life. Although they are naturally aware of our every nuance and have great insights into us, we must learn for our part to trust and love them.

This means making an effort, not so that they grant us three wishes but so that they are rewarded for their unwavering care. It means creating a space where the Guide can come through and be present, thus fostering the relationship of intimate friends who do not just turn to each other in hard times.

The Guide must have an affinity with the person he or she is working with in order for the best possible outcome. Therefore, the person will naturally feel a connection and empathy with the Guide, so making a warm friendship that much easier. It is highly unlikely that the Guide would show himself in meditation as a soldier when the person involved is a pacifist! The aim of the Guide is not to be provocative or to bring about a moral conflict, the aim is to appear to be in sync with the person. As the Guide is 'in spirit' he or she can adopt any guise they please to appear the most appealing in order to do their work more harmoniously with the person. However, they may just appear as themselves in their most applicable incarnation. As all incarnations are only masks or roles for the soul, I suppose we could assume that any guise the Guide adopts is a mask. When a soul is naked, or 'in spirit' then the material, manifest desire to wear a recognisable form is removed. They will wear one for us to relate to more easily whilst in their realm they are effectively bare-soul naked.

There are several categories that Guides may come from. In my work I have discovered that the main ones appear to be connected by either earthly ancestral links or by soul-type or species. Firstly, the ancestor Guide will be a relative of the person involved. This would normally be a relative who they had known manifestly who had subsequently passed over into spirit. The bond there is strong already and a link of earthly love still connects both Guide and guided. However, this should be questioned as there are two problems here. On one hand, it should not be dismissed that the person had another Guide before the ancestor Guide was able to step in and the likelihood is that the original Guide was not ancestral. The second issue is, as the Guide had only recently been deceased, his or her links to the manifest will still be relatively strong.

The necessary balance between manifest connection and spiritual connection may not be achievable.

Recently deceased members of the person's earthly family may make loving and attentive Guides but they lack the detachment of being effectively removed from the manifest. Therefore their wisdom may be impaired by the vestiges of earthly emotion. They themselves may still be locked into their own earthly role, their incarnate state, and so they may have regrets and desires still clinging to them. Time in the Otherworld to acclimatise and adjust, regaining harmony and balance is more appropriate before an ancestral Guide steps in.

There are two more things to bear in mind...one is that we are dealing with a soul, a human soul, whose wisdom comes from being able to see the bigger picture from a perspective of both the Other Worlds and the Earth in unison. However, they are still a soul which was recently housed in mortal form and I do not think that we would expect anyone to go through the death/after-life trauma only to re-adjust immediately and 'get on with the job', as it were. Also, the person involved may be mourning for the departed soul for some time and seeing their dearly loved family member as a Guide rather than Mum or Uncle Ted may be impossible. Then the temptation would be to relate in an Earth-bound way and not to respond to them as spiritual beings.

It is sometimes hard for us to remember that our parents, when they pass over, become free souls at liberty to incarnate again into any role they choose.

This issue was hard for my partner Robert. I had to pass on guidance to him that his Dad had chosen to incarnate again and was no longer 'in spirit' to be contacted. We can easily assume a Christianised concept of our departed loved ones floating about as Mum or Dad in Heaven, waiting for us.

Indeed, we may be reunited in spirit, but in spirit the need for those roles is no longer there. Love between souls is strong and cannot be diminished by this loss of the Mum or Dad persona. With ancestrally linked, family orientated Guides we should try to relate to the soul for its enduring characteristics and traits rather than by its previous temporary and manifest condition.

Guides so often fall into this category of those with whom we have an ancestral link but that link is more effective if the spirit has been passed over for some time...say a Grandparent who died when the person was young or an Great-Aunt who had passed over before the person was born. It can be comforting to know that our Earth-relatives still love us and are keen to see us have the best possible outcomes. It can remove any fear of the Guide relationship and can make for a satisfying exchange with its foundations based in a family lineage. This, to many, is a strong link and the family is the foundation for all security and love. What of those who do not feel this connection, either because they had a rather dysfunctional family, a small family or an unhappy time whilst in those circumstances?

If Guides were only forged of ancestral spirits then many of us would go without, and this is not the case. It would not matter that Great-Great-Great Grandpa John wished to Guide someone if that someone felt no warm connection or positive links with their current incarnate family. The person would not particularly warm to the idea of the Grandpa figure as Guide as their would be too many negative associations attached.

What of those who have a great love for their parents or family but who feel no spiritual tie between them? Our parents are, after all, individual spirits come together whom we chose to be born through into the world. There is no reason why the souls involved should have bonds or connections beyond the manifest needs of all involved. There can be earthly love but no soul-link and in such an instance the ancestral Guide would not make much of an impression. The person would be more drawn to a Guide of similar soul-type, especially if people of this soul-type were lacking in the person's life.

A soul species, type or group can be explained by example. In the work of Doctor Arthur Guirdham, a man who had first-hand experience of the patterns of reincarnated souls, he was aware of a group who came together at various periods through history. These people incarnated at the same time and would be drawn together by events in order to live out their lives in unison. This goes beyond the simple soul-mate connection where two compatible, kindred souls will come together in countless incarnations to learn life's lessons in tandem. This is a group of people who share the same type of essential Self who harmoniously gel and bond in order to support each other in life.

Thinking of this scenario in childish terms may help, in considering what a person really is...what is inside the person? As a child, we may have perceived humans as types of animal, seeing some as squawking birds, slimy reptiles or cuddly little mammals. This experience is often repeated when an adult takes hallucinogenic drugs and perceptions alter to see people as 'they really are' (which can be as animals, goblins, demons or any other permeation the imagination can conjure). The point is not that we are all really animals. We cannot incarnate into an elephant's skin, or into the form of a bird because we do not know how to be elephants or birds, only humans. So it is with the soul-type, one sort of soul-being cannot incarnate into an incompatible form. The many types of soul can be perceived as different liquids filling the vessels of bodies. One would not pour tea into a wine glass, nor beer into a coffee mug. In basic terms you cannot put a lemonade soul into a soup bowl body.

I do not claim to know how many dozens of soul species there are but if they follow natures pattern then there are undoubtedly many sub-species of the root type. This must, according to natural law, be constantly evolving and to try and list the types would be redundant. Far better as an exercise to use the imagination in a childlike, free fashion to perceive the difference for yourself. Giving humans attributes can be a good way of sharpening intuition and heightening perception. Even if the person we are looking at is not really an owl-type or an elf-type, we are seeing beyond the mask and considering what type of soul the person has.

The Guide who comes from the soul-type will appear as an archetypal figure or easily recognisable image. This does not mean they will appear as a God or Goddess form... a Guide will not take on the powerful energies of Herne the Hunter or Athene the Lady of Wisdom and Creativity. The intense energies associated with these Deity archetypes would overwhelm the natural energies of the Guide. Effective communication would then be impossible as the naturally compatible flow of energy between Guide and recipient would be perverted by the huge Deity vibrations of that archetype. If a person encounters Deity form in a meditation then it is safe to assume that either the archetype is true or else a spirit with no particular form or personality of its own has taken on the shape. If the latter is true there is only a limited time that such a spirit could deal with the energies involved without collapsing in on itself under the pressure. Stringent tests should always be performed on anyone, but anyone, who appears in meditations and astral work.

To 'check out' or to reveal the true and genuine nature of a spirit, all that is needed is to hold up a mirror to reveal their true essence or soul-type. This, or a personal variation on the theme, should always be used without fail. This goes for meeting the Guide, of course, as the Guide is the prime target for being emulated by another 'mischievous' spirit entity. How immensely satisfying and nourishing it is for such a nomadic entity or thought form to be related to by someone as a Guide! Always check out your Guide, no matter how well you know them. They will not be insulted ...rather they will be pleased you are being sensible!

Rogue spirits are frequently, if not exclusively, from the human astral, cosmic debris which causes much trouble. This will come up later in the book as we continue to consider the many spirit forms we may encounter.

The soul-type Guide will probably have been incarnate and it is possible that the person may have once known the Guide incarnate, in another life. Most Guides have not been incarnate for some time, having devoted themselves to spirit-time and the helping of others. They have the balance of human/spirit right and so can relate with the wisdom of a distance between their own soul and the earthly matters that come up. This does not mean they are unemotional and disinterested in our petty lives but it does give them a clarity and uncluttered perspective, free of personal needs and desires relating to Earth. In my case, my Guide has always appeared to me as a Native American man in his middle years. He is no Shaman or warrior, he is very simple and ordinary. I found his clichéd appearance to be annoying and then amusing. Why should my Guide be another Native American? How twee! How very predictable!

I challenged him about his appearance and it's meaning. Obviously I put more emphasis on this than he did, being discarnate and less interested in appearances and bodies. He had been in this form, in life many centuries earlier and he had enjoyed the form. He chose to wear it primarily because when I had stopped being grumpy about the fact my Guide chose such a hackneyed image I actually liked it and could easily relate to him in that mode. Besides the 'fashionable' aspect of the Indian way, it was true to say that my Guide had picked a guise that would not upset and irritate me. His mode was not meant to distract or to cause me any unease and his was one of the few modes that I did not find intimidating in some way. He was not making some statement about his Native American-ness. My Guide is a discarnate soul who was once an Indian in one of his lives but who is now only wearing that set of clothes to give me a character to relate to. He is of my soul-type and one of our ways of being is the Native American ways. The issue of him appearing as a male will be looked at in another chapter. For now I can say that obviously all souls can be male or female, they are complete in themselves and can express themselves equally as either gender.

Once a soul is in spirit, discarnate, it can wear whichever guise suits. Just as on Earth, once we incarnate we choose the gender most suited to our life's journey and lessons. In spirit, one is a balance of the sexes, sex is not an issue without the body and the body is not in spirit. Emotionally, intellectually and spiritually our souls are not about male/female or any other manifest denomination as regards gender, race or creed. In spirit, all is equal.

The Guide chooses a mode to appear in for a reason and they have to 'wear' some image for us to recognise them. We, as manifest beings, need to interact with a Guide in a way that can be related to manifestly. "My Guide is a Red Indian" works far better than "My Guide is a purple miasma"!

Besides the Guide of our soul-type there are those which are forged of past-life links. The story here tells of one such Guide.

The Story of Andrew

Andrew is a man in his early thirties who approached me, asking if I would discover his Guide's identity for him. I told him that I would do this on the proviso that I could teach him how to work with the Guide on his own. I do not like telling anyone what they are, what they have been or who their Guides are. It is disempowering for them and they are in danger of believing someone without any first-hand knowledge themselves. Most people want me to tell them and they certainly do not wish to do any work themselves. I do not admire this attitude although I can understand it, being born of an 'instant' age in which we absorb all information without much of a thought about how genuine it is.

I could have had all sorts of hidden agendas when I told Andrew the identity of his Guide and I could have been very unethical indeed. The typical thing that I could have done is to assess his character and to give him a Guide which I know he would like and enjoy...in his case it would have been easy knowing his interests and hobbies. However, I had no intentions other than to speak with his true Guide and then to tell Andrew how to do the same. I did a meditation to discover his Guide's identity.

His Guide turned out to be Allyson, a feeble and poor girl who had known him in another life. In meditation I contacted her and she told me her identity and who she had been in Andrew's past life. He had been Vincenzi, an Italian monk who had come on a mission to England. He had stopped at the Abbey in the North where she had been as a young girl.

I gathered she had been there in a perfunctory capacity, being milkmaid, cleaner and general dogsbody to whoever needed her services. Her Father had been a minor landowner and had passed her on to the Church, as she was not marriagable and was not bright enough to be a nun.

Allyson had become besotted by big, dark Vincenzi who seemed less boorish and brutal than the other religious men she knew. He seemed genuinely holy and she idolised him. He in turn felt sorry for her and was strangely attracted to her pale and thin appearance which was so different to the Italian women who seemed big and brash in comparison.

One thing lead to another (which it does, even for monks!) and they took to taking moonlit strolls miles from the Abbey. On one of these walks Vincenzi and Allyson lay together and she became pregnant. Vincenzi left the Abbey, oblivious to her condition, and made his way south.

Allyson, pregnant, undernourished and pathetic, made her way on foot to where she thought Vincenzi was. She did not know what else to do except find him. He was the only one who had ever shown her any kindness. She located him at a church in Winchester, away from the cathedral. When Vincenzi saw her he was overcome with fear and remorse. On learning her condition he struck her about the head. Allyson, being the size she was and in such appaling shape was killed quickly and simply by the first strike of his large hand. Terrified and distraught, Vincenzi had bundled her limp body into a cupboard-sized room under the stairs and left her there until nightfall. He then retrieved her body and made to bury it outside the church wall.

Allyson, as a spirit Guide, did not acknowledge that he could have buried her outside the wall and maintained that he would have buried her inside, under a tree. The images she showed to me told me differently. Vincenzi then left the country in a hurry, traumatised by his horrible act.

Andrew was not expecting to have a poor waif of a medieval maid for his Guide, it did not suit his persona to have someone so dull and plain. When I read him the guidance I had been given, however, it struck a chord with him and he became upset and quite involved with the whole thing. I was worried that he did not want to understand the process, only the result and he began to rely heavily on me for more information.

I had said I would teach him how to find Allyson for himself but meanwhile he pestered me to find out more and to fill in all the gaps for him. I was also concerned that Allyson was too far immersed in her role from her past-life to be a focussed and true Guide. She still referred to herself as Allyson and to Andrew as Vincenzi which made me think that there was little hope of her guidance being of any substance. She appeared too Earth-bound and far too connected to her last incarnation. I was surprised to find he had a Guide so locked into a last life as I had not expected such a thing to be possible...yet I knew to expect the unexpected in all psychic work. I did all the necessary checks and Allyson was indeed real and true. Her concern and love for Andrew seemed to be paramount to her and she told me she was his soul-sister, caring for him.

I was not used to a Guide talking in such terms, my own Guide was a spirit of great profundity but not much flowery talk. I thought it was high time Andrew talked with her on their own level as my soul was not akin to hers and communication was not difficult but it did not flow between us.

I tried to give Andrew the tools to meet Allyson as his Guide, in meditation. Using a simple relaxation technique of slowed regular breathing I lead him into trance. I gave him the imagery to draw a protective silver circle around himself which he could then draw up to make a shield all around him. I suggested he should put on a protective suit of silver which I allowed him to visualise and eventually imagine himself wearing. I asked him to see himself holding a symbol of protection, be it the mirror mentioned earlier, a ritual knife, wand or pointed stone. These should be used as a means to ascertain if any figure coming into his created space was who they said that they were.

As this was to be his created astral corner or the Other Realms then his laws were to be obeyed. Anyone having the protective item held up at them must reveal their true shape and thus be banished or spoken to accordingly. I spent time talking Andrew through his sacred landscape, where he had chosen to stand in his protective circle. This included sight, sense, smell and hearing to create a whole picture of his sacred environs. It would also help him stretch his psychic skills a bit, to add noise and scents to his place of resting.

I encouraged him to have representatives of the four elements in his landscape so as to create balance and power. Ahead he must see a representative of the Earth, a mountain, green hill or rock for instance. To the east, on his right he must turn to see the air having an effect on his realm, behind him perhaps the sun was shining and to the west as he turned again there was water. He now had the four directions to refer to and give his place more form and energy...and his position in the centre symbolically meant that he was in the best place to receive guidance (the space-between-the-worlds, the ether, the cauldron or the womb-void). He was ready to draw another silver circle outside of his own and to invite his Guide to step into it.

Andrew had seen all of the other things I had asked of him in his minds-eye and was ready to see Allyson his Guide. He drew his astral circle and invited her in. This was unsuccessful. Andrew had no faith in his own Sight, surely anything he saw would be false, he would be making it up?

I could not convince him that his vision would be no less effective than my own. He had followed exactly the same guidelines as I used and so he would get results. I suggested that he practice this and be patient. She was there, she would appear.

Andrew seemed more than a little obsessed about her appearance and I think he was put off by the fact that she was such a puny creature. He would have found it easier to have envisaged some stereotypical buxom medieval wench as this image was already in his library of consciousness, to be called upon. I tried to explain that Allyson was a soul and that her 'shell' did not matter. If he could not 'See' her clearly it was of little consequence as long as her presence was in the circle. He must rely on his own intuition and Sight for that, which I knew he had and could use. The repetition of the meditation ritual to get to the sacred space was too boring for him to wish to go through time after time in order to meet the Guide.

Andrew wished to try other methods...he wished me to try them. He wanted me to do automatic writing and a ouija board. This was the point at which I bailed out, getting increasingly annoyed by his laziness! In retrospect I cannot blame him, again he is used to the instant world where information is given, not worked for, not questioned. I felt sorry for Allyson who was waiting for him to talk to her in a tried and tested way, yet he never did. Before I left Andrew entirely to his own devices I gave him some details of the places in Winchester involved in the demise of Allyson. I had been given these details in meditation by Allyson's spirit, in order to convince Andrew of her validity. They did indeed check out as real and geographically sound details, I having never set foot in Winchester had no idea if this, I just passed the guidance on to Andrew.

Andrew intended to go and look around the place to see if it stirred anything within him. I do not know whether he went or not, but no doubt if he did then he expected a multi-coloured, *'Fantasia'*-style revelation. I do not say this in criticism, I cannot blame Andrew as the victim of a fast-moving world where computer graphics are often more visually appealing than nature itself.

I find it sad that he and many like him will turn away from magic and psychism as they do not provide entertainment that one can turn on and off. They do not produce puffs of smoke, stars and beautiful manifestations. Being a Witch is not a glamourous thing to play at being, it is not 'performance art'. It is hard work, often in isolation. Not everyone can do the work, Andrew obviously felt he could not, although I felt otherwise. He had the creativity and the imagination. He had an interest and he had a devoted Guide keen to talk to him. By the very fact he had asked me in the first place to identify his Guide shows he was alerted to her presence. Yet he would not devote his free time to an activity that was laborious and produced few spectacular results.

I personally do not see that anything could be more worth time, more wonderful, than speaking with a spirit who resides in another Realm. They are your personal link to that Realm and others, they have chosen to be with you. What could be more special and amazing?

There are people I would help without expecting them to do any work themselves. In Andrew, I saw possibilities and I felt his latent psychic abilities. If he wasn't a Witch he could at least learn some of the ways as he had the hidden capabilities to some degree. Also, he actively wanted to know, it had come to the forefront of his psyche and he pursued it. Other people have no natural inclinations at all. They will never be psychic, although once in a while the odd psychic phenomena may cross their life-path. Their having the occasional glimpse of the Spirit Realm does not make them a psychic/Witch anymore than my knowing what a ballcock is makes me a plumber. Shaun was one such person who asked for my help but who was never going to be able to do the work for himself.

The Story of Shaun

Shaun told me that his house had suddenly become 'haunted' and could I go to the house and somehow exorcise it? As I believe that most hauntings are no such thing (as I will go on to discuss) I went along to Shaun's shared, rented abode prepared for almost anything. I was met by one other resident, a woman, and her two friends who were sitting in their car outside. They would not go in as they were too scared. They described the usual litany of smells, noises and moving objects that go with most cases of spiritual interference. These can be frightening, as I know from my past experiences of being bombarded by such events repeatedly.

I felt on familiar ground with the usual set of 'poltergeist' style behaviour in the house. They obviously had a psychic disturbance but to label it as a ghost...a dead person's spirit...was a little hasty. There are so many other things that it was more likely to be. The number of dead humans whose souls feel so bound to an earthly place that they stay there after death is few. Once dead, a human soul tends to have only a temporary interest in the world it has left behind. There can be some sadness and lingering regrets but usually the shifting out-of-body is such a liberating and joyful experience that the soul moves with the flow away from the manifest. The freedom in losing the body-shell does not inspire the soul to remain in manifest realms. Suddenly all such worldly worries seem meaningless when faced with the peace and wholeness of the bigger picture.

The only way a soul normally stays 'in situ' is if the death was so sudden that the soul does not realise it has died. The jolt out-of-body is so instantaneous and unexpected that it can take some time for the soul to become re-orientated. The shock and violent trauma of such an event can disturb the spirit and it can remain trapped near to the spot it can relate to from its last memory of life. This can either be the entire soul or a fragment of it, which can be retrieved and re-integrated with the rest of the soul by a psychic. Psychic soul-retrieval work is practiced for any form of trapped soul energy. It is usual for a soul to linger around the scene of its death for a short while, observing but the Guide will come when necessary and lead the soul away. This may be more difficult for the Guide if the soul is traumatised by a sudden death. A soul is never abandoned by the Guide. It will need healing before it can make the journey. . Ghosts really are few and far between, in the true meaning of ghost as human soul.

Shaun's house did not have such a ghost. A couple more options open were that either one of the house-mates had 'picked up an astral bug' in the form of an unwanted collection of human energies. The other was that the placement of the house itself or else the energies of the actual building were having an astral shake-up. This could mean that circumstances activated the energies of the site or area on which it is built or excited the very fabric of the house itself. Either way, this will trigger old events and experiences stored in the land or the building to be replayed. Earth and stone store memory and this memory can be replayed with extraordinary effects. It is difficult to convince someone that the house is not really occupied by the ghost of a Roman centurion, however the land was once camped on by the character and his resonance, his vibration is being seen and felt. Played back like a cosmic video recorder, triggered by a psychic mood or electrical disturbance.

In Shaun's case, it was not this option. Rather, his boyfriend had picked up an astral nasty, a cosmic germ, and had brought it home with him.

I sat alone in meditation on the landing of the house and felt no human presence, only a vague uneasy shifting of some energies behind me. I located the source of these energies which came from above the lad's shared bed. As soon as I tracked the energy it shifted next door to the girl's room. Protecting myself from psychic intrusion, I pursued it, trapping it into a circle of power. Thus held, I asked for it's purpose. I was dealing with an energy which was so unformed it had no shape at all. It was a thought-form of human origin, based on sexual desires. The boyfriend of Shaun had been subjected to some rather lewd thoughts of some intensity at a party, I discovered by questioning this astral pest. I was told by my Guide, as the thing was too ill-formed to communicate except by its crude means, that it had grown in size by feeding on the sexual activity in the shared house. This centred around the lads and the girl in her room next door.

The sordid little thought-form had also perversely fed on their fear of its leering presence and had got an inflated sense of its own importance. It took little to send it packing, off to the place in the universe where it may receive healing to be cleansed. It was such a stupid and horrible collection of energy that I found it easy to banish. Trying to explain this to Shaun and his friends, who had expected a ghost or apparition and much exorcism was another matter.

I decided on honesty. As I explained my understanding of the 'presence' Shaun gave me confirmation that the trouble in the house had not started until the boyfriend had returned from a party some weeks earlier. I feel the gang were a little confused by my discovery and subsequent clearing of the energy but I was told that it worked. I felt that somehow Shaun was disappointed by there having not been more drama in the story but the girls were relieved. The one whose room had been plagued was grateful to be rid of the 'dirty, smelly old man' feeling she had felt watching her.

Shaun was a factor in my next tale which is an account of other types of spirit form that one may encounter. It is the role of the Witch to help, but helping one's self is always hardest.

The Story of my Flat

It was my flat, a purpose built affair in one of the best roads in Bath. It had a glorious view of the city as it was up on one of the hills that surround that splendid place. It was inordinately cheap for such a property and had apparently been impossible for the agents to rent out. Judging by the beauty and quality of the accommodation I had no idea why. We were told by the landlord's agent that an old lady had died in there and since then her daughter had been trying to rent it out.

Myself and Martin, who was still my partner then, were prepared for the residue of the presence of an old lady. We did not expect her ghost as such, merely a resonance, a vibration or her last years there alone...perhaps a sadness or loneliness, a feeling of gloom? We cleansed the flat thoroughly before moving in, both astrally using a visualisation technique and manifestly by simply ripping up the old carpets and decorating. Furnishings can hold astral debris and feelings and we wanted the place to be ours.

Whilst decorating we got some feelings about the two bedrooms at the far end of the flat, which appeared somehow darker and more unfriendly no matter how brightly we painted them and how much we cleaned them. We supposed that once we had moved all our own things in the place would feel more like our home. However, this sense of being at home was never realised in those particular rooms.

Due to this intuitive sense of discomfort we decided to sleep in the living room instead of either bedroom. We used of the bedrooms as a guest room and one as a study for me to do my art and writing work in. Somehow we couldn't bring ourselves to sleep down at the bedroom end of the flat. The living room had a big window and a balcony looking over Bath and we pretended for a while that our logic was that we wanted to wake up to the view. However, it became increasingly apparent that we had company of a spiritual nature. which was centred around the two rooms that we instinctively avoided as much as possible, especially at night.

As Martin and I were so close and both as psychic as each other we both knew what we could feel was correct. The feelings scared me as they were very hostile, occurring mostly after dark and with a distinct 'get out!' sort of message. I could get no clear answer as to who or what was residing in the 'bedroom' end of the flat.

The intrepid Martin spent a night in the 'guest room' in the dark trying to commune with the presence, but he said it kept shifting about from bedroom to bedroom. It clearly did not wish to co-operate. We did a mediation to speak to the old lady who had died there but found that her soul was long gone and so not responsible for our disturbances.

In our separate meditations we did gain some clarity about one of the vibrations we were feeling. The flat was built opposite to some huge old houses with enormous gardens. They were obviously the properties of those with considerable financial means. Martin and I were both told individually in our meditations (without the knowledge of each other) the story of a Victorian woman who had come from one of the houses to meet her lover on the land our flat was built on. This land had been an orchard during her time. She had, in time honoured tradition, fallen pregnant and been locked away as a mad woman in her own home. The image of her being fed laudanum stuck with both of us and it seemed as if she did indeed go mad. Her insanity pervaded our flat some-how, even though she had never physically lived on the land there. Again, she was not a ghost, haunting the spot of the lost love but somehow her unhappy and confused vibrations still remained for us to tune into.

Still this did not explain why our flat felt increasingly uninhabitable and hostile after dark. Some nights the black, ominous feeling reached the living room, our 'retreat' and it was all that I could do to stop myself grabbing my bag and running out into the street. The message from the bedrooms was undoubtedly 'get out'...the 'it' responsible had claimed its territory and effectively declared a psychic war upon us, the intruders, as it saw us.

The war was waged by night. The bedrooms were never so bad by daylight and I would work in the study and change in the spare room in those hours. However, on the one occasion I was so absorbed in my work after dusk that I forgot to leave, I was rapped on the head by an invisible presence.

I was, frankly, terrified as this presence was in no way pleasant. It wanted me out of its territory. This was the singular most 'solid' physical contact I have ever had from any spirit or entity and sadly it was a hostile contact. If that touch was formed from words then it would have been a scream of anger. It wanted me out of its space, it was dark and so it was claiming its territory.

The accompanying stench that this presence possessed was the singularly most vile and potent aroma I have ever witnessed from 'spirit'. The smell was thick and 'real', it was cordite or gunpowder. Gradually the 'bedrooms' smelled of it constantly sometimes so sickeningly it forced me out of the area.The rap on my head was accompanied by this smell and also an image. It was that of a mutilated soldier, more dead than alive. This was enough to keep me out of my own rooms for some time.

Martin was determined to sort out the presence but in each meditation we did, or in each ritual banishing he attempted, we were illuded. If anything the presence grew more inky and all-pervading. It began to enter the living room at night,

Martin saw it as a black shape-figure standing over us and I woke to the feeling of being observed coldly on most nights.

Other people began to become involved as we alone could not cope as this was our home and we were too close to the matter. We looked to others for advice or suggestions but once people encountered the rooms they did not come back. Two friends, practicing Witches, went down to challenge the 'thing' that was making our lives miserable. Although confident that they could deal with spiritual intruders, they were terrified by the presence and they spent the rest of that evening in the living room. When they bade farewell that night it was for the last time as they never contacted us again. Such is the power of fear and the problem of those who are afraid somehow blaming the psychic for attracting the thing in the first place.

There is a feeling that the attracting of presences may be contagious and so the psychic is effectively 'quarantined'. This also illustrates the difference between the Witch (traditionally speaking) and the Wildwitch/psychic. Not all Witches feel the need to believe in phenomena of a supernatural kind as such events do not touch their lives. These non-psychic practitioners of the Craft deal with the energies and forces of the Otherworlds every time they enter into ritual or magical acts. Yet as they never hear, see or feel anything 'real' associated with such spiritual endeavours they do not pursue the active contact with Spirit that the sensitive Wildwitch does. I am not concerned with the traditional side of Craft-Witchery here as I believe enough has already been written about it. I use this point to distinguish the actual difference between those who are born into the psychic Witch role and those who chose to operate as Witches for their own reasons.

A Wildwitch has no such choice to be or not to be. In myself and Martin's cases, we could not help what we had 'awoken' in the flat as we could not repress our inherent natures.

The presence had grown so strong that even non-psychics could detect it. A friend of mine who was, at the time, sceptical and impervious to atmospheres, a woman of hard fact and science, stayed the night in the guest room. She awoke to find a six foot spectre in white looming over her bed. Meanwhile, Martin and I roamed the streets on many occasions being driven out by the extreme malevolence of the vibration in the flat. It was as if it filled up with a grim ooze which had no heart or soul. Martin and I both began to see the place as a graveyard and thought it was high time we looked to move. It was such a beautiful flat in the daytime it seemed a shame but we were losing too much sleep. A creeping void was gradually beginning to consume the flat and there was nowhere left to hide from it. We were at a loss as to how to relate to such an alien atmosphere, devoid of any human attributes.

In the meantime we checked the library for old maps which may give us a clue to the land use of the site before the flats. It had apparently never previously been built on and had indeed been an orchard for some time. We checked the register of owners of the flat and found an unreasonably high turnover of tenants in a short space of time, ending with the death of the old lady. We came to a dead end in our investigations and with our attempts to work with the place psychically. We were clueless.

Our letting agent, on one of his visits, had commented on the burning smell. This is the cordite 'emission' from the supposed bedrooms. The smell was becoming so 'actual' that a completely non-sensitive person could smell it. I believe he secretly took us to be closet pyromaniacs but as we were nice quiet, rent-paying tenants the agent let it go. The flat, however, was beginning to actually manifest its presence, through our psychicism. It was using our open 'channels' to come through into our world from its astral one. The likelihood of two open practicing soul-mate psychics moving into such a place was slim. I do not know why we were there as it surely was no positive thing that we were inadvertently assisting the manifestation of this cold, desolate energy.

We were saved from any further attempts at solving the flats labyrinthine mysteries when Martin bought the narrowboat and we moved out. I was very sad to leave despite the terrible feelings that emanated from the flat. It had been our first home together and I had so wanted it to have an atmosphere as beautiful as its positioning and views. For all its newness and besides the fact it looked nothing like an archetypal 'haunted house' it seemed to be impregnated by negativity.

Some may attribute these difficulties to the emotionally hard times that Martin and I experienced there. Yet we had been very happy together when we had moved in and still the flat had a 'life of its own'. Martin believed the flat to be some sort of spiritual vortex, a place where there was a tear in the fabric between our world of the manifest and the others. Strange things leaked through, no doubt drawn to and feeding from our own open psychic energies. It seemed such an unlikely place for such a tear to occur, in the bedroom of a purpose-built flat! However, was it any more odd and weird than Martin and I knowing each other in medieval France? Maybe not. I know that I do not know and therefore I will accept the unexpected.

In conclusion to this rather inconclusive story, Shaun was someone who shed some light on the matter sometime later when I had moved out. He said his Father was a military man and that as a child Shaun remembered being taken inside the very hill that my flat was situated on. The hill was hollow and inside there was much covert activity. He described a labyrinth of tunnels and offices and recollected with a lingering astonishment that he had actually seen large vehicles being driven under there.

Shaun said this infor-mation was for my ears only. I hope it will not affect him that I have shared my findings here.

Shaun had not been back there since his childhood visits and he had no more to tell me except that the site had been one of the many where a battle had been fought around the Bath area. I think these two snippets are enough to explain the disturbed and negative vibrations which affected us there. We were effectively connected by bricks to the energies of violence and destruction, soaked into the land and there to be tuned into by sensitive people. The combined effects of both the hollow hill full of military activity and the land having been fought on in past wars was enough to create a distinct resonance.

I feel sorry for that beautiful flat and I often ponder its new tenants. It is no wonder that we could not cleanse it or work with the intrusive energies. They were not energies of individual spirits but one huge force, an emanation from the terrible and pitiless war machine in its various forms. It was no wonder that we could not relate to the effects it caused in a sensitive human way as the very concept of war cannot be conceived of in such a fashion either.

Psychism and Witchery deal with so much more than the stereotypical ghost hunt. The energies involved in spiritual disturbance can be subtly different and each can require a new approach. Flexibility and going with the flow are again essential. A rigid attitude which states "Oh, I know what this is!" is bound to be blown away with the next strange exper-ience.

There is pleasure in helping people and in getting involved in the mysteries of the energies which connect everything, all of us. The Guide, the Witch's best friend, is an integral, vital part of the process of discovery. The Guide should be worked with at all times, no astral work should be attempted without consultation with this most trusted companion. The Guide has no big ego-trip, no ulterior motive. He or she will give you the bigger picture and the best course of action to take for the most harmonious outcome. Even if it is not what one wished to hear. As with the Guide, their unexpected guises and their unlikely advice we must be open and ready to consider the unorthodox. If we do not, we will only hear what we wish to and disregard the rest. We will risk becoming narrow, stunted and effectively dead to the energies. Energies cannot flow through something so impermeable.

Discover your own Guide, remeet them without prejudice or expectation. Let them take you through your own unique, wonderful web, your personal sacred dance. Go with them into the Otherworld and bring back guidance for the good of those who ask. This is the role of the Wildwitch.

Chapter Four

Soul to Soul

The Stories of Suzanne and Lindie

Being a Wildwitch and natural psychic is about helping others, pure and simple. Suzanne was a friend who needed such help as her problem was obviously one of the psyche...a soul problem. I say this because of her description of what her life was like.

Suzanne's life should have been one which brought pleasure, fulfilment and excitement as well as the exhaustion that she constantly experienced. She was working as an advertising consultant for an established company in London and in such a capacity she was challenged on all levels and kept extremely busy. As a counterpoint to this intense intellectual and practical stimulation, Suzanne had a wide social circle and was booked up for months ahead of herself by friends wishing her to attend parties or meals. Despite such success socially and in the office Suzanne was deeply unhappy with herself for no reason she could pinpoint in her daily life.

To observe the independent, successful woman that Suzanne was when she was at work or with friends one would never understand the problem. Looking at the manifest situation there were no indicators of any aspect of her life which would be causing her such inner discomfort. Indeed, to talk to Suzanne there were no signs that this unease stemmed from her childhood, which she discussed fondly, or her early adulthood which she recounted in amusing anecdotes and stories. The only actual physical clue to Suzanne's difficulties was in her spiritual questing. As a sensitive woman, she realised that her problem was deep within her own soul. Consequently she was desperately searching for truths to shed light on her internal unhappiness and discomfort.

Her chosen spiritual searches ranged from crystals to Reiki healing to auric cleansing to chinese medicines. Suzanne usually attended these sessions only to be filled with an overwhelming sense of disappointment and depression afterwards. Occasionally, the words of one lecturer would stick and she would live her life according to their 'regime' for a few weeks but then Suzanne would become deflated and unhappy again. None of these people solved her inner problems or remedied her deep-seated fear for long. Suzanne felt alternately confused or even more humbled that she somehow was not able to absorb wisdoms given to her.

Besides the physical clue of Suzanne's searching of new age philosophies there was another less obvious clue. Suzanne seemed to be particularly linked to her friend's partner who was herself a psychic and healer. Suzanne spoke of this woman in a mixture of awe, reverence and dislike...but she always spoke of her, pre-facing many of her sentences with "Mandy says..." or "Mandy thinks that..." Apparently, Mandy the friend's partner had once incorporated Suzanne into her psychic healing group. Suzanne had tried very hard to get Mandy to alleviate her long-term sense of failure and inadequacy which held no basis in physical truth. She wanted Mandy to 'tell her how it was' and Mandy was more than happy to oblige, in fact she had been happy to entirely take over from Suzanne and do all of her thinking for her. For a while, Suzanne enjoyed being taken over and told how to see things and how to think. She had liked Mandy 'looking after her' and being concerned enough about her to be her psychic protector and champion. Mandy was adept at convincing Suzanne still further that she could not trust her own psychic feelings and that she needed someone stronger, like herself, to lead the way.

After a while, Suzanne grew uncomfortable with the crushing weight of Mandy's knowledge and views upon her. She was torn between breaking free, and losing both her friend's support and Mandy's, or giving over every last shred of herself to float along in Mandy's strong current. The first option meant Suzanne being alone with her own fear again. Yet surrendering her will entirely to another adult seemed equally frightening on an intuitive level. As Suzanne was fully operational both at work and with non-psychic friends, she could not be an entire and successful individual in one sphere of her life and a mute puppet in another. This division between her capability as a practical woman and her seeming inability to believe in herself made Suzanne more exhausted and more ill.

The more run-down Suzanne became, the more outside spiritual help she sought to get her better, and so the vicious circle was established. Mandy was able to step in and tell her that only she could make her better if Suzanne would only do what she said. She did everything to play up Suzanne's fear of her own judgement and did an efficient job of almost disempowering her completely. If she had succeeded then the efficient practical woman who went to work and socialised would have collapsed also. As it was this never happened as Mandy went too far.

As it appears to be with many psychic or sensitive individuals who allow their ego to be their driving force rather than the need to help, Mandy fell prey to a lower astral thought-form being. This piece of human cosmic debris was attracted to the idea that it could feed Mandy's ego by giving her nonsense psychic messages in the form of supreme knowledge. Like so many others, Mandy was fooled by the piece of astral junk which had formed into an entity conning her weaknesses into believing it was a supreme being and she was a 'chosen soul'. It fluffed up her already fattened ego and told her that she had been the incarnation of many famous people, amongst them, naturally, Christ. Playing further on the power dynamic of the situation, the nasty little thought-being intimated that of course Suzanne had been Judas!

Now to you or I this may seem either very sad or easily explained as archetypal/symbolic role playing...which has its own soul- relevance and can explain a soul-dynamic. To the two people in this scenario it was entirely serious and to be taken literally as a past-life revelation. Mandy was open wide to anything that would further inflate her self-importance as some sort of latter-day psychic saviour and Suzanne was equally open to being told that she was indeed not very good or trustworthy and she certainly needed some one to guide her fully.

In this instance, the entity cleverly added in the Jesus/Judas scenario that Judas should feel guilty and somehow beholden to Christ. So Suzanne was indebted to feel such feelings towards Mandy, further strengthening the link. In addition, the friend of Suzanne was brought in as another disciple who stuck by Jesus, therefore making Nancy more elevated and Suzanne more ashamed.

Having witnessed many individuals with Christ-complexes, most of them sadly in my work with mentally ill adults, I realise the power of such archetypal imagery and energies. People need a purpose bigger than their own. Not only that but they need the suffering/martyr aspect to make sense of their own painful lives on earth. In the West, Christ-consciousness and Christian imagery are potent and resonant forces to adopt. To Mandy, herself a respected professional person, it was too tempting spiritually for her to deny intellectually. However, Suzanne's 'work-self', that whole, functioning and capable Suzanne-part thankfully intervened on the behalf of Suzanne-the-damaged-and-headlocked-soul.

As Suzanne had not irradicated her practical intellectual work-self, that self then immediately stepped in and said "No!" Suzanne could not allow herself to believe that she had been Judas. She could not feel it, it did not 'belong' to her. She could not relate to it on any level and her manifest and successful self would not settle for it as a truth.

As soon as she questioned this supposedly awesome piece of cosmic information she broke some of the link between herself and Mandy. Suzanne told me how when she had broken away physically by refusing this concept of Jesus/Judas, she had felt extremely ill to the point of vomiting. The sickness was the result of 'casting out' the unpleasant connection she had with this domineering entity.

The image of this lovely and intelligent woman being sickened by the force, effectively heaving up this influence, is not a nice one. It serves to re-illustrate the imperative need we should all have to protect ourselves from unwanted astral attachments. The world of psychism is not a 'fluffy' one, the nasties are all out there. Of course, Mandy for all her 'wisdom' did not ever tell Suzanne to protect herself. Mandy was supposed to be Suzanne's protector...why protect herself from Mandy?! If Mandy had truly been a friend and spiritual teacher to Suzanne, her first advice would have been about Suzanne learning how to protect herself psychically. Also for Suzanne to learn how to contact her Guide in order to do her own psychic work and her own validation of cosmic 'truths' such as the proffered Jesus/Judas snippet. Why did Mandy not do this for Suzanne? Can we conclude that if Suzanne was kept in ignorance and fear that she would be reliant on Mandy to provide the information and validation? Can we assume that if Suzanne had been given the knowledge of how to 'check out' guidance then she would have checked out Mandy's as bogus? Not only bogus but potentially damaging?

Suzanne 'saw' clearly once she had symbolically 'vomited out' the residue of this unwanted influence. Her own latent psychism came back to the fore and she knew what was happening was wrong, very wrong. She felt abused and hurt by one she trusted and she broke away from the situation.

In so doing she managed to do two things. Firstly, she reactivated a past-life link to Mandy. As long as Suzanne had been playing along with her, Mandy had been 'dormant'. As soon as Suzanne said 'enough' then Mandy's old patterns of behaviours reactivated and Suzanne, her friend and Nancy stepped back into a past-life drama of energies.

Secondly and ironically, this triangle drama was exactly the cause of Suzanne's seemingly ingrained malaise and self-doubt and its reactivation was to prove the eventual cure for her ills. However, getting to the point where she was 'cured' was to be very unpleasant.

Suzanne began to suffer psychic attack from Mandy, Mandy being extremely displeased to have had her Christ-self rejected. She effectively removed herself and Suzanne's friend from Suzanne's life which obviously hurt the sensitive woman. However, Mandy continued to link with Suzanne via insidious psychic intrusions, playing further on Suzanne's insecurity. This ultimate aim of this was to lure Suzanne back to the benevolent and efficient Mandy who would say "I told you you needed me. Only I can tell you". However, all Mandy succeeded in doing was making Suzanne more afraid of her and also more repelled. Suzanne tried once again to find an answer in spiritual teachings. As most 'alternative' therapies of the type that Suzanne sought do not tend to dwell on the negative aspects of psychic communing then they cannot have been of much assistance to the frantic Suzanne.

The Suzanne I saw was exhausted both by sheer physical effort and by her being attacked constantly by Mandy in a more etheric way. Both her manifest energies and her spiritual energies were low and the idea of her being able to see anything clearly in that depleted state was unlikely. With her permission, I asked if I may look into the causes for her feeling so useless and inadequate when in reality she clearly was efficient and well-regarded.

Suzanne had desperately wanted someone to help her. Being psychic oneself, as she clearly is, can be no help when one is too close to the problem to 'see'. I myself have sought out her help when I have had personal problems which she could deal with as they were not hers. Psychics and sensitives know the difficulties of gaining true guidance for themselves as wish and will, personal assumption and delusion, can so easily cloud a view. A psychic can 'see' and pass on information without judgement or personal interference for others, if not for themselves. This can be very frustrating indeed! Suzanne needed unbiased and fresh overviews that she was too close to get for herself. She did not need for me, or for anyone, to 'tell her how it was' or to dictate exactly what she should do. Knowing the nature of guidance as something which can be unexpected, obscure, symbolic or any combination of 'weird', she had been nervous of asking for it, exhausted as she was already, both psychically and emotionally. I could not, obviously, intrude into Suzanne's astral airspace until she had given me the go-ahead. This would be totally unacceptable. So I offered my services and waited to see if she would need them. Yes, it was hard watching a friend chase her tail and suffer but I could only offer and wait, anything else no matter how well meaning would be yet another intrusion for her to deal with. After all, Mandy too was 'well-meaning'... in her own unfathomable way. How dare I assume that my 'well-meaning but uninvited' was any more worthy that another's?

To see what I could find out for Suzanne I followed the usual pattern for gaining psychic clarity-:

a) Sat in comfortable quiet space, not having just eaten as to be too 'grounded'.

b) Drew my protective symbols down over me and imagined I was sitting in a circle of protective blue fire.

c) Imagined I was wearing my protective, reflective silver 'mirror' suit/garment.

d) Visualised myself in my safe place.

e) Called for the Guide to appear in a circle of blue flame.

f) Tested the validity of the Guide by pointing and asking.

g) Asked the Guide to take me to the place/time/space where I may best gain understanding of the specific problem (i.e. the recurring difficulty that Suzanne has with confidence and self-worth)

At this point, I was taken to a 'scene' by the Guide where I watched an 'astral movie' with a commentary. This was visually very dynamic and affecting. However, it is not my preferred form of receiving guidance. One can so easily forget details when trying to remember afterwards and sometimes one can miss big pieces of the action when trying desperately to store minor facts one may have just witnessed. Far better for me to receive guided writing with accompanying symbology. In this instance I watched the 'film' for the overall picture and subsequently went back to get detailed written guidance for Suzanne.

The story itself is personal but the essence of it was one of slavery and power tripping, of revenge and subjugation. Mandy's soul had linked to Suzanne's in a 'master and servant' scenario. Mandy's soul had become so used to this power-play that it was more than a little reluctant to relinquish its grasp. Even though slavery, thank the Goddess, is a thing of the past, the bondage link was strong and resonant in their soul-patterns. I asked why had the soul of Suzanne never broken free of this terrible binding which chained her to Mandy's will, forcing her to play out her part? The answer was that Mandy's will was strong but it was not unbreakable. However, the soul of Suzanne had gradually become so damaged and conditioned over the centuries that she did not know how to be any other way. Nor did she have the first idea how to incarnate if it was not in one of these scenarios. She had thought that she could somehow win out over her if they kept playing this game.

Of course, the only way to win was to stop. I asked my Guide why the Guide's of Suzanne and indeed Mandy had not intervened to stop this waste of time? Apparently the Guides had this time around and that was why Suzanne was seeking help and wanting out. The Guides could only intervene if asked for, if required. They could advise and offer help, but they are Guides ...they guide they do not steer the ship. They show you the options and then step back. However, it had been strongly suggested that the scenario should end now and so the energies of the situation were changing at last.

After I had returned to my safe place and thanked the Guide, I left meditation and grounded myself by writing the whole episode down as fully as I could. By the time I went to make a cup of tea and to phone Suzanne with this information I realised that by connecting so strongly with her in meditation I had picked up her problem. I could actually feel the misery and despair that Suzanne carried with her on a daily basis. On phoning her, I described the symptoms that were upon me, a need to weep and wail, a hollow feeling of being nothing, nobody. Suzanne did indeed begin to weep on the telephone and confessed that she did indeed feel these feelings and it was killing her soul and will to go on. I said that we could solve her problems but that she would have to help me and work with me actively to banish Mandy's influence once and for all.

I said to Suzanne that, with her permission, I would pursue the question of what she may do to sever all ties with Mandy. I tried, with permission, to protect Suzanne astrally whilst she worked through the betrayals of the past and the pain of the present. I called her up onto my astral safe place and I guarded her astral bodies with blue fire. I also 'de-corded' her aura (etheric body) repeatedly to get rid of the astral arrows/links that Mandy fired at her. Guidance gave clear written details of an effective and active banishing ritual that Suzanne herself must undertake. The event was to be a physical affair, undertaken at dark moon when the energies would be appropriate. Suzanne was to banish the links for herself, in a structured but personal way. She must chose the setting and the tools.

Banishing completed, this was not the end of the matter. Of course, Mandy as a psychic felt the astral vibration of her being 'turfed out' and she came back with both astral and manifest fighting. The astral arrows were met by a united front, both Suzanne and I astrally blocked her subsequent attacks.The previous patterns were indeed hard to conquer and Suzanne found herself more than once slipping easily into letting others 'know best' and relinquishing her control with a familiar feeling of fatigue. This mode was her way of being for so long that is is obvious that she may be inclined to adopt it. This does not mean that as soon as she did, all links with Mandy were re-established. Suzanne was finally aware, actively aware, of her predeliction for thinking herself rather useless and furthermore she understood it. That very personal and real understanding could never be born of someone merely telling you 'how it is'. Suzanne had to hear the guidance personally and be confident then that she could proceed with knowledge and wisdom and opposed to ignorance and fear. She embraced her own psychism and intuition as a reality that she could trust.

I included this tale as an illustration of what souls are capable of, the damage that can be done, the patterns that can be forged. We cannot label Mandy 'evil' for surely before her incarnation as 'Boss' she had repeatedly experienced her own pain and warping to make her so twisted a soul. No soul is made evil, the actions may be a result of some damage to the eternal being which causes us to view them as such. All damage can be repaired, over time, if the soul is made aware of the harm it is doing.

Like Nazi officers carrying out atrocities, the soul can be convinced it is acting for the best, because it is right to do so, no matter how appaling the act committed may appear to a more informed bystander. I only hope that someone is given permission to reveal to Mandy the terrible harm she is inflicting on others as a result of her own soul-injury. Until then, we sent her healing and have a faith that those in the universe who are assigned to protect and Guide her will be on hand to help her soul more fully.

A sad twist to this tale is that Suzanne and I did not speak to each other for a while as I made a mistake. I offered her a piece of unsolicited guidance. There was no intention on my part of trying to control Suzanne. Having so recently felt her suffering and helped her understand it and be free of it I hope that I was more sensitive than that. But the lesson for me was that any unasked for intervention, no matter how 'well intentioned and innocent' is an invasion of an individual's space and privacy and therefore as insulting as any genuine manipulation.

The next story I will tell to illustrate a point is about Lindie, a woman who I never met. I was given a photograph of her and told of her problem and asked if I could help in any way. As I had no personal contact with the woman I had to do all my connecting with her on the astral levels, with only a photographic image as a talisman. Without that image I could not have done the work. I needed some connection to her and the resonance of an individual can be held just as adequately in a photo as in a personal item. The art of divining clairvoyant information from a personal item (psychometry) is quite different to the Otherworld interactions which I myself use. An image of the person is all I really need to hold with me as I travel into the realm of the Guide.

The information that I picked up astrally about Lindie was not very positive. In fact, a tale unfolded before my eyes that made me feel such sadness and anger as to weep for her poor soul. This did not bode well for passing on guidance to her...if I, the Witch, was so affected by the information then what effect would it have on Lindie herself? I spent some time going back into a meditative state in order to check and re-check the story I was being told and shown, but there was no escaping the fact that the events depicted had indeed shaped the current day Lindie and were highly relevant.

Lindie would have to deal with the information if she were to tackle her current problem and I could not get around the fact that I would have to tell her. I wished heartily that I could be some comfortable old Granny Wisewoman dispensing pleasantries about 'tall, dark strangers' and 'travel overseas' at that point! Who wants to get guidance that they have been raped and driven to madness in another life..the aftershock of which was still hurting the soul? Who wishes to hear that the family which she held so dear had been involved in this past scenario and were now trying to atone for it?

These are the things I had to try and get across to Lindie. I had to try not to alienate her with a flood of negativity yet I had to depict the story as I had seen it, not pleasant at all. I don't know what she was expecting from me but I am certain that it was not what she received.

I used the same pattern for my meditation but I had pen and paper along side me as I sat so that I could take down 'automatic' guided writing at the same time as being shown imagery in the trance state. This may sound hard...and it is! The writing flows out spontaneously, usually in the direct speech of the Guide or sometimes in the voice of the person I am getting guidance for. Pages and pages are filled, the writing often sprawls everywhere in a frantic attempt to get it all out, get it all down. I am usually surrounded by a mountain of pages with scribble at all angles all over it which I then have to decipher. I am fairly used to my Guide's way of speaking on paper but any 'newcomer' speaker may flummox me with their style or form. The words are usually a commentary to the images I 'see' which helps bring them to life further and makes sure that I recall everything afterwards.

I have no idea at all at the time what is being written as I am too absorbed in watching the images before my 'mind's eye'. Although this method is somewhat frustrating in the aftermath of sheets of scrawled communications, it is also my preferred method as imagery alone cannot provide such insights. I am given imagery and I can then put my own interpretation upon it to some degree. With this method, having the commentary along side the pictures I am kept more to the point. I am given facts, names, dates etc where relevant and usually given some snippet that the person seeking guidance can research for themselves.

As I have previously stated, such 'facts' are not necessary. I do not need to 'prove' each case I tackle as being 'genuine'. The only validity for me comes from the patterns and energies that the past-life scenario, be it real or symbolic, reveals. The 'facts' help the person I am working on behalf of feel involved as they the can be the one to do follow up research. In other instances having 'facts' makes the person give more credence to the guidance. They may need validation even if I do not. As with the case of Andrew that I referred to in the previous chapter, people are trained to expect results. Most of us are geared to count success as the acquisition of concrete evidence, not the subtler images and patterns that psychics are used to working with. I cannot expect everyone that I do guidance or psychic questing for to work on the same subtle level as myself.

I will now share with you the story I was given about Lindie as it makes a pertinent point to refer to afterwards. The story begins when I am shown Lindie as a young woman. I always try to remember that yesterdays young women may have looked quite mature when in their twenties as life expectancy was considerably different. I would estimate that Lindie was barely past her teenage years when I observed her in my trance state although her bearing and gait made her seem quite middle aged.

The setting was medieval and certainly European. I was given a repeated image of Lindie as this young maid walking up and down, up and down a long corridor with a book in her hand. She seemed unhappy, intense, lonely and worried. Every time I attempted to 'tune in' to Lindie's soul in meditation I got this same picture of her pacing the corridor and I felt a sort of reluctance to go any further. I got a strong sense that this was a key moment in time just before a more unpleasant event, and to some degree Lindie's soul was indeed still pacing this corridor, up and down, before the next cataclysmic event occurred.

I knew I had to force the scene onwards although this took some will as Lindie's soul (and my own) did not wish to see what happened next. I was given some background inform-ation through spoken guidance. Lindie was of reasonably wealthy stock, her Father was not rich enough to wish to support his rather eccentric and withdrawn daughter and so had passed her off to the manor of a considerably more wealthy couple. Lindie had there become a glorified lady in waiting to the obnoxious and demanding Lady of the house. The father was only concerned with money and position and paid no heed when Lindie protested that she wished to become a nun and leave the house. In fact, Lindie's father was little concerned with his daughter at all as he had precious few thoughts for women, considering them to be rather pointless unless at his bidding. He conveyed this attitude strongly to the Lord, a coarse, domineering and brutal man who then observed that he could indeed do as he pleased with Lindie with no protest from her father. The father was but a sycophant to the Lord.

Lindie, being female and unwed in those times became vulnerable, unprotected. Yet she still had an amazing aura of self possession and power. She said little, did as she was bid and spent her spare time reading her prayer book in the vain hope that one day she may be admitted to an order. She persisted in being unflirtatious, disinterested in male company and in wearing fashions that had long since dated. I saw Lindie in a ridiculously tall hat and a plain dress, a very austere and odd looking figure with a haughty and aloof countenance. She must have indeed cut a strange dash as she paced the lonely corridors of the huge house each afternoon, reading and remembering religious texts! The ridicule or abuse she sustained did not seem to reach her and as she did her tasks well and was not unruly there could be little real complaint.

This rather dreadful life could have continued for Lindie had it not been for the Lord. It was winter and he was bored. Lindie had begun to catch his eye repeatedly. She stood out as the only one who would not flirt or fawn to him and her silent subservience both annoyed and aroused him. He began to desire Lindie, not in a loving way or even in a sexual way but in a way that wanted to crush the silence from her and to crack her shell of reserve. He wished, in short, to have her and break her. The Lady noticed the Lord's attentions drifting again and again to the peculiar Lindie and was not pleased. She decided to put an end to Lindie's piety and purity...two aspects which no doubt titillated the Lord. She plotted to send two guards to remove Lindie from her constant lonely pacing one afternoon and take her away to do their work upon her. That would stop Lindie being quite so fascinating to the Lord...indeed, it would make her a ruined woman. The Lady too wished to break Lindie.

Having received this background information I could appreciate why Lindie was reluctant to go beyond this scenario of pacing a corridor. It represented to her eternal soul a time when she was left alone and could keep her dreams of being a nun. She may have been unhappy and terribly isolated but at least she had still had her pride and dignity and her hopes intact. At the moment when the guards enter the picture to remove Lindie from her corridor then all that she had was taken from her. I believe a part of Lindie's immortal soul fragmented at that point and remained 'in situ', i.e. eternally in that corridor. That would lead the current incarnation of that soul to feel bereft in some areas of her life, perhaps emotionally. Certainly she would be experiencing blocks of a personal nature as her soul was incomplete and hurting. I needed to 'see' why Lindie had been so scarred, although the thought disturbed me greatly. I had to understand the scenario in order to re-integrate or retrieve that lost part of the woman.

In brief, Lindie was taken by the two guards to a small chapel or ante-room well away from any other person. There they undressed her, abused her and raped her in turn. Throughout all of this, the being taken and the attack, Lindie remained silent and stared only at the ceiling as if she were willing herself out of the experience. She offered no resistance or no protest. For the guards, although they did their loathsome duties which the Lady had paid them for, this was unnerving and made them feel less than lusty. With no struggle and no pleading, Lindie became just some strange mute doll who exuded an air of such silent madness as to be rather frightening in herself. The guards may have felt that she was more frightening than them and they soon abandoned their task and left her alone and naked on the stone floor.

I myself 'saw' the hours go by into darkness and observed Lindie's twisted face staring blindly at the roof of the chapel building. There was such pure despair and probably the start of mental illness there that it was very painful to observe her. I felt utter horror at the scene.

There was a woman dispatched from the Lady to make a show of finding Lindie that evening, pretending that all had been worried about her disappearing. Lindie allowed herself to be moved and dressed and fussed at but she would not speak. From that moment on, Lindie was completely silent no matter what occurred. I believe that she knew who was responsible for the loss of her dreams and for the loss of her dignity but it no longer mattered to her. Lindie was effectively killed off that afternoon although a person in her form still walked about, ate and slept. I believe that is why the image of her pacing the corridor is the last cohesive one Lindie has. Perhaps she was consumed by a mental illness immediately. Perhaps she did not fully ever comprehend the meaning of such violation.

When a soul is so traumatised it is not possible to gain much more insight other than by observing and speculating for one-self and by asking the Guide for clues. Lindie's soul had undergone such a blow as to be very damaged and twisted even today. She had obviously had healing and love whilst in the Otherworlds as a deceased spirit and she had clearly chosen to incarnate again to put it right, but the damage was quite bad. If one hears tell of the rest of Lindie's incarnation after the rape then it explains still further why her soul may be in a state of dis-ease.

The Lord had been furious at what had happened to 'his prey' Lindie and immediately knew it to have been the work of his smug wife. He, being the most immoral and selfish of persons had her poisoned. No one dared point out to this wealthy man that it seemed a little obvious that his wife had been murdered as they were all frightened of him and reliant upon him. Like all men in his position no matter what he did some people could see no further than the length of his title or the size of his money bag. The Lord waited no time at all before claiming Lindie and installing her in his bed. He too found little sport in her silence and insane staring and before long the only pleasure he gained from her was to beat her. She was tied to his bed for days, emaciated and bleeding, but no one dared to challenge him.

Eventually she was with child, which she lost due to her pathetic physical and mental state. It was after this that the Lord discarded her. Remaining in the house for several days Lindie was then left alone and unguarded as she was now a bit of a pointless puzzle that nobody knew what to do with now the Lord did not require her. Left alone, Lindie took the opportunity to end that appaling situation and she threw herself from the window to her death.

What was the point of all this for Lindie? Why did she need to experience this terrible drama? And why had it come back to haunt her as part of 'guidance'?

For Lindie personally, the needs of her two brothers in this incarnation had brought her back to put the scenario right. They had been the two rapist guards paid to torment her in that life. Their needs to put things right and to be loving supportive men in Lindie's life were being blocked by Lindie's subconscious revulsion and hatred of what they had done to her. They needed her to forgive them whilst she did not wish to remember in order to forgive. I do not believe for one moment that the brothers consciously knew they had raped Lindie in another life. Their soul agendas dictated that they must atone for their damage but they as manifest humans did not know or understand. Lindie did not remember consciously but her soul agenda was to block out any reminder of this harm that had been done to her. So the dynamic of souls had been set up whilst the conscious adults knew nothing of the underlying energies...hence why Lindie had been referred to me with a family problem. Her sisters were also involved as past life associates in that incarnation...probably fellow maids who did not support Lindie. The whole of these characters had come together to 'mend' Lindie. My task was to allow Lindie the conscious choice to see what energies were causing problems. I wrote down all I had seen, hard as it was to tell her of such terrible events, and I tried to explain as best I could why such resonant past-life energies were at work today. Everyone around her was trying so hard to make amends with her soul yet she needed to remember why and decide if she could forgive this time around.

I did not tell Lindie that she must forgive. When such a grievous harm is done to a soul then it may take many centuries and lifetimes to get around to wishing to make things whole again. Perhaps Lindie was on the path to this recovery but not quite ready in this life to fully absorb the full implications of the past-life trauma. The brothers (and, indeed, sisters) needed her absolution immediately in order for them to feel better and more capable of moving on. How much easier is it to ask forgiveness than it is to truly forgive?

I do know that Lindie was more than happy with the guidance that I came up with for her. I was worried about her response to such crushing past-life information as I did not know the woman and was not there on her doorstep to support her.

However, the energies involved in that centuries-old scenario made clear sense to the modern day Lindie. She could gain an understanding of the patterns that were affecting her present day family and with her new informed standpoint on the past-life links involved she could see to make more appropriate decisions. It is not mine to know whether Lindie is ready to forgive those who helped warp her eternal soul through their own greed and ignorance. I was able to give her the insight to base her own future decisions on and that was all that I could do. I could not save Lindie although I felt for her. My job as Wildwitch is to provide a relevant part of the bigger picture via my Otherworld links.

I did have to ask Lindie's permission to heal and retrieve her missing soul-piece. Had I have had 'access' to her in person I would have guided her back during a regression so that we could retrieve her own soul-part in situ and she herself could be active in the process. As it was, Lindie was not available for 'hands-on' work on a one-to-one basis. I would advise this close personal work wherever possible. However, in this instance I could work on the astral on Lindie's behalf with her permission. I knew that I had to go back into my meditation, with my Guide, and to approach the 'Lindie' who was stuck in the corridor, pacing. This is where the Guide is invaluable (again!) as such soul-work is a delicate process. My Guide had brought Lindie's current Guide along to help take the lost soul-part along to the astral space where it may best receive healing and gentle re-integration with the main incarnate soul-part. A painful and poignant task.

So, why had Lindie's Guide allowed for the soul-fragment to be wandering in torment in another time? Two possible reasons. Firstly, a Guide can only do things with our invit-ation and permission. They can suggest ideas to our psyche but if our psyche blocks the idea through pain or fear then the Guide is not able to progress. Secondly, the soul-loss of Lindie had to alert her that something was currently not right...missing...from her current life. This nagging feeling eventually lead her to seek help from me and to deal with the energies relevant to her patterns and relationships today. There is never a wrong time for anything...including soul-retrieval. Everything occurs when it should do in order for maximum learning to happen.

One issue that Lindie's past plight brought up for me was that of how many souls have been (inadvertently) damaged by societies' disregard of the female sex. Again, to bring up the Nazi analogy, the Nazi's seemed to genuinely have an understanding that the Jews (et al) were not human and therefore did not require humane treatment. In other words, the Nazi's justified their actions by feeling justified...the Jews were inhuman and therefore could be disposed of, used and abused as any inanimate soulless object could be.

This argument has been transferred to the animal rights debate. If an animal is soulless (and therefore inhuman if we assume only humans have souls) then it can be treated on the same level as any other item designed to aid and abet man...basically on the same level as anything else a human owns....car, house, clothes. An animal, to those with this belief, is something that is useful to humanity and if it outruns its use it can be traded for the next disposable creature and killed off.

To put oneself in this headspace is to begin to gain understanding and empathy for those who are ignorant and fearful of the truth. Such people with similar ways of thinking cannot be branded evil if one truly attempts to understand that they believe that they are right and justified. This applies to all those souls who have used and abused and disposed of the female gender throughout history. I will not excuse these acts of rape, torture, murder and violence but I will attempt to comprehend. As I observe the souls of Lindie's brothers...essentially sexless eternal souls with the capacity to be either male or female incarnate...try to make amends to Lindie's soul then I witness the greater pattern at work.

We can all incarnate as male or female and in any number of scenarios and settings. We can be told that it is a truth that women/Jews/gays are evil and should be exterminated. We can be brought up in a regime or in an environment that convinces us this is right and true. We can all learn soul lessons in understanding in this manner, being the victim in countless lives or indeed the persecutor. It is when we refuse to learn the lessons contained in these life dramas that we cause the real harm and damage to wider circles. Our actions radiate out with repercussions down the years and as we know and so we cannot claim that our lack of understanding causes no harm.

All of our energies effect countless other souls. We can either take responsibility for our thoughts, actions or deeds...or not. It is when we choose deliberately to refuse to see the real truth or to face that we have done real harm that there is the potential for evil. Evil in definition can only be said to be the knowledge that something is deeply harmful and damaging but the choosing to go ahead and act anyway. This is not the ignorant belief that one is right and proper to kill Jews as they are verminous animals. This is the knowledge that of course this is not the case but why not go ahead anyway?

This translates across to the treatment of the female sex in society. If one has the knowledge that a soul can potentially be male or female and that we as individual souls may be male or female in their next incarnation and yet we still persist in hurting women for being women then we are being extremely foolish and playing with fire (as a cleansing, transforming energy as well as that of anger). In the opposite capacity (and there is always an opposite capacity!) a women who persists in the thought pattern of 'all men are bastards' whilst under-standing that she too as a free soul could have been a man or may be one again is setting up a spiral of negative and damaging energy.

In our society today we repress and pervert the sacred Goddess and God energy just as adequately as we ever did during the dread years of the middle ages and Christian tyranny. The terrible legacy of this shows through in our stories of reincarnation down the ages although it manages to escape all but the most pertinent historical texts, texts like that of 'The First Sex' by Elizabeth Gould-Davies (Penguin) which is a highly recommended but thoroughly harrowing read. Repeated tales of rapes, burnings, mutilations, removal of rights and properties scatter any selection of past-life recalls. Souls incarnate have seemingly always had a hard time as a woman and what has changed today?

We incarnate now into a society which reveres youth, is repelled by flesh that is not taut and honed, and which sells images of such youthful glory in every conceivable situation. It is hard to find anyone who is not under twenty five years of age and under ten stone in any magazine, cinema advert, television commercial or newspaper promotion. The vast majority are not represented and in some cases their images are positively repressed as being fat, ugly or old. Women again are those who come off worst, up against a society which positively encourages that we punish ourselves for not being young and slender. Not only that but we bring our children, male and female, newly incarnate souls into a visual age where they may see a bottom shelf newspaper of an almost nude woman in a provocative pose next to a comic of their own choosing.

Pornography spills over into all of our lives and gives out messages and energies which perpetuate the tyranny of centuries earlier. Certainly, those who get paid to exhibit themselves thus are not exploited victims. I do not mention these energies in modern society as a crusade for those who have chosen a female incarnation to be seen as victims at all. Neither do I accept that those few young women who sell their bodies in any number and manner of ways are somehow revered and honoured. Their appeal and the admiration that they receive is not based on anything but a transient facade. True worship and love of the female form is not confined to a glossy young female sexuality. It moves with that sacred Goddess energy and reveres the woman as she moves through the tempting dance of youth through the strength and creativity of motherhood and into the power and wisdom of the crone. Yet our reverence, our overwhelming visual homage,stops as the feminine image moves from the breath of spring into the ripe fecundity of summer and autumn.

The repression of the mother and crone aspects of Goddess/female energy in society is dangerous for us all. Just as much as the treatment of woman as male commodity was in the time of Lindie's medieval incarnation.

I do draw attention to the role that we all play in condoning this repression of normal, healthy and vibrant energy of a female nature. As everything is energies and our energies are everything we cannot abstain from this depiction of the female in society. We cannot be personally absolved from any responsibility. If we claim to have any understanding of spirit and incarnation, as Witches or no, we cannot put the blame on men...as we all have male potential. We cannot put the blame on 'them' as we could all incarnate as 'them'. We are one another. We cannot be separate from the pornography and the naked young ladies selling cars printed next to a story about famine or war.

The point is that we may lament over Lindie's pitiful tale and rejoice that such repression and abuse no longer exists. The energies have shifted but the patterns still remain. As we have observed with so many other aspects in this book, we know we can affect change by one question, thought or deed.

Firstly we must see that pure sacred woman energy is being perverted and denied. In seeing this all around us we may understand that we are still out of balance.

Energies, especially that of the Dark Goddess, cannot just be hidden or locked away without effect. A repression of Her power as Great Mother or Grandmother for the sake of youth and beauty is to disrupt the sacred balance and to ask for an eruption of negative energy patterns. The flipside of the Goddess's strength and power is uncontrolled rage and a repression of this translates as depression and despair. We must begin by re-addressing the balance within ourselves, male and female incarnate, by no longer seeing ourselves purely as one gender or another. We are soul. We are soul wearing a guise, a chosen energy. We must not blame the other, denigrate the other, repress an aspect of the energy which is not camera-perfect. Only then do we stand any hope of creating a world into which we may incarnate as people rather than a set of genitals. Only then do we truly avoid another Lindie scenario.

I am guilty of the repression and fear of female energy. I have always felt myself to be strongly male in energy, but wearing a female skin on this occasion. My interests and feelings are quite 'male' in orientation and my creative drive replaces my maternal one. I had no understanding of how I could be positively female incarnate as all my female incarnations had been unpleasant due to male intervention and disruption. I thought it best to be on the side of the aggressor, as it were, and to reject blatantly female energies.

I see now that this rejection of the feminine was part of my residual fear again, fear of being hurt at the hands of men as I had been so brutally across the centuries. I did not wish to be made vulnerable as a mother or lover, I spurned any role which laid me open to male abuse.

I was pleased to have a male spirit Guide in the form of the Red Indian who I loved and trusted infinitely. I knew I was going against the gender I had chosen to incarnate into but I saw strength and power only in male figures. A female guide would have had no authority over me. This is sadly how I felt until my Guide thankfully decided I needed to learn.

I met my Guide as usual in meditation in my safe place and found that he wished to walk with me a while. He took me on a journey which involved a short boat ride to a familiar part of my 'trance landscape'. Here he dropped me off with several women who I had chanced upon before in meditation. One of these appeared as an elderly lady and the other appeared as a purveyor of specific Goddess qualities, more a set of energies than a woman. These two stood at the mouth of a cave and welcomed me. I was a little confused as to why my trusty Guide seemed to be leaving me with two women figures. Although I liked them well enough I wished to remain with the solid and secure male figure of my Red Indian male. Yet he was adamant that he must leave me for a while with the women. In fact, they were to guide me for a while. I became a little concerned and begged him not to leave me. Although he assured me he would return one day, he told me firmly that for now I needed to learn to trust in the authority of those with female energies and forms. He would return when I had accepted this and learned from it.

My two patient new female Guides took me then on a journey into the cave labyrinth, a place where I understood women had met to celebrate womanhood for many millennia. At the time I had no book learning to back up the matter, I took their word for what I witnessed there. They lead me to the heart of the labyrinth where there was a 'womb cave' and there they left me with the sounds of the sea all about me and a hole in the cave roof by which I may observe the moon, the eternal representation in the heavens of the feminine principle.

I was afraid of such isolation in the spirit-realms at first, especially without my trusted male Guide close to hand. I felt alone and vulnerable surrounded by female energies and women-forms. However, as I relaxed, which it was impossible not to do in the moonlit cavern with the sea swishing gently around me, I began to understand the mystery of being in the womb-void for the first time. I started to relax into the great privilege that it was to incarnate in female form, with the potential to create new lives, new dreams. My initial time with both Greatmother-Two-Moons, (my new Guide) and Hera (the Avatar of the much misunderstood ancient Goddess) was both scary and hugely enlightening for me. I certainly was not prepared to reject their kind offer of love and guidance and so my only option as a Witch on my path was to open up to their wisdom and to be taught.

I fought against it, for sure, initially convinced that being a woman meant little more than being a downtrodden second rate citizen. If that was the case then I would surely get second rate and feeble guidance? Yet those two great spirits proved from the outset that their spiritual depths were like the labyrinth that they lead me down initially. I was so ignorant when they lead me there ...so much so that I knew nothing of the Greek Deity Hera or of the tradition of using caves as places sacred to the Goddess! I only found that information out later from research, which of course validated all they had told me.

My only knowledge of using caves came from my past-life memories of being part of the Mithraic cult, that great predecessor of Christianity, which again worshiped and revered a male deity. I obviously had much to learn and a great deal of conditioning of my soul to unlearn with my two new wonderful women-formed Guides!

I am eternally grateful to my Red Indian Guide for placing me in their care and beginning my own personal lessons as to the validity of female energy and the ultimate importance of treating all as a soul, not a gender. In this chapter I hope that I have made the point of our soul relations being so much more than enemy/victim, male/female. The stories here seek to go some way to illustrating soul-patterns and links across the years and how these energies and patterns affect us down the centuries (or across them) in all manner of fascinating ways. Other lives and other selves have their own agendas and it is these varied, colourful and complex roles that I go on to explore in chapter five.

No one dwells in isolation, no man is an island, in fact, no man is just a man! We could all be anyone, and we probably have been...

Chapter Five

One and All

"How many lives can there be in one universe?
....One!"

Richard Bach from *'One'* (Pan, 1988)

The next tale I have to tell in connection to the complexities of soul-relations is that of myself and a lady named Ruth.

Ruth was Martin's wife in this incarnation, before I met him. When I first laid eyes upon them both as a couple I was aware that not only did I recognise him from a previous incarnation but I also recognised his wife. This was not a joint recognition, I realised that by some enormous cosmic coincidence that I also knew Ruth from separate encounters.

Although the overwhelming urge at the time was focussed on my being with my 'soul-partner' Martin again, I was still fascinated by my recognition of Ruth. As an issue apart from the dynamics of the situation of the time, I felt uncannily wary and yet simultaneously in awe of the woman. I did not share too much of this with Martin as he was busy with his divorce and with the practicalities pertaining to any separation. Not only that but we had so much of our own soul-business to catch up on that it would only confuse the issue to suddenly bring his ex-wife into the arena! Yet I could not get Ruth out of my mind.

I knew this was not just a matter of she and I locking psychic horns over the 're-allocation' of Martin's affections. Although I was aware of Ruth being a renowned Witch I realised it wasn't just her current cosmic attentions that I could feel.

I knew that she had desired the divorce in order for her to have the freedom to leave to be with her own soul-love and so the amount of hostility towards me, Martin's 'new' love, should have been minimal. Yet I still felt Ruth's spirit breathing down my neck almost constantly. I began to feel almost haunted by her presence, by a 'ghost' that was very much living! I could not help myself but I had to ask Martin as much as I could about her, which was not what he wished to discuss! The more I heard about her the more I realised that this link was absolutely nothing to do with the present situation we were in but it stemmed from another time when we had met, soul to soul.

One afternoon, Martin and I had to meet with Ruth and her partner to discuss fine details of the divorce. As soon as I sat down opposite the woman I began to acquire a migraine headache. Sadly, this eventuality is not such a unique occurrence for me, although this migraine was on the wrong side of my head to its usual position. Migraines are often attributed to psychic energy which comes to the surface very rapidly but is not allowed to find an exit or an expression. I tried in vain to rid myself of this pain but found instead that I began to retreat into it and actively hallucinate. Anyone who suffers from this type of migraine will be aware of the 'out of time' feeling one gets in accompaniment but this was combined with a spiritual input.

As I sat at the table I began to drift off and see myself and Ruth in another life together. I was clearly seeing myself standing in a vast hallway admiring Ruth's collection of magnificent oil paintings that lined her staircase. I knew that Ruth in her current guise resided in Martin's modest cottage and so that the home I was 'seeing' was a dwelling from another time. I became aware of myself as Ruth's maid and I knew that I should not really be idling on the stairs but at work in the kitchen. There was a sense of anxiety at being caught in admiration of her possessions. I was drawn to going up the stairs, instead of back to the kitchens,and I found I could explore the quarters and floors of the house that were previously 'banned' to servants - unless they were accompanied or went about their duties extremely quickly. The memory I was experiencing was accompanied by my 'owning' it - I felt the feelings of that maid, I was her. This was no pain-induced thought-rambling.

All this was happening while I sat at a pub table opposite Ruth! Eventually the ever-attentive Martin realised that I was 'gone' (into spontaneous trance) and he gently helped me to regain clarity and to ground myself. He also began to attempt to heal my migraine. At this point I had to confess to a curious looking Ruth that I had just had a flash-back of our previous incarnation. As I described her house to her I saw her glance at her partner in acknowledgement. I told her of the paintings and of many other details in her large house and I revealed I had been there in the capacity of serving girl.

Ruth looked taken aback but not too shocked. She and her partner confirmed that they had indeed been incarnate many years previously in such a house and that I had witnessed what they themselves had 'seen' psychically as their past dwelling. They were both initially thrown by my obvious psychic ability to tune in to such matters as well as they themselves could. When this primary amazement had worn off I could see that they were a tad smug that I had once been their servant! This did not bother me at all. I realise that I have been a servant on more than one occasion and was later to realise that I had indeed been Ruth's servant on several of those occasions!

I do not know how my free-spirit, my restless and subversive soul, dealt with such sublimation. Maybe it tried to teach itself regimentation and discipline as a balance to the wildness of its natural way. Perhaps my soul liked being told what to do for a few incarnations of rest from being the lone renegade or scapegoat. Whatever, it did not concern me to have been Ruth's servant and the discovery of such pleased me. At least I now knew how I recognised her, primarily it was from the life when she had lived in that grand house with her partner as her then- husband.

That evening Martin noticed that on my temple where the migraine had previously manifested, there was a graze and a bruise. As I had not manifestly hit myself that day we knew the wounds to be psychic impressions. Martin suggested that I tried to go into trance again to witness how I had come by these wounds. The feeling was that my meeting with Ruth had triggered the initial recall of that past life and so this old wound had followed. What was its relevance?

In my meditation/trance I allowed Martin to guide me back to the point where I was in the house of Ruth again. He did this by gently suggesting visual cues that would evoke the previous clarity I had achieved that afternoon. As the whole connection was still fresh I had little trouble in slipping back into the memory. What I discovered was that I had been hit with a candlestick as punishment for snooping in Ruth's rooms. Ruth herself was a woman taken to disappearing for periods of time from her house, at liberty to do so as a wealthy woman. I was tied to the place, young and restless and with an overwhelming urge to see 'how the other half lived'. I think I had rather admired Ruth at that time and I'd wished to enjoy what she enjoyed. I wanted desperately to see her things and admire them.

As she had gone out on the occasion in question, I immediately went unobserved to her private suite. I must have lost all sense of time as I wandered about and looked in drawers and opened doors. Before I knew it, I was being attacked by Ruth who had returned to catch me in the act of snooping. There was a hard blow to my temple with a candlestick and then there was no memory.

That night I dreamed a little more of the story. From that point on I had been partially sighted. I had been of a relatively philosophical and positive nature in that time and had accepted my punishment duly and got on with my life. My respect and admiration for Ruth did not diminish as I had seemed to have been of the opinion that she was my better and that was that. Yet her feelings towards me turned from ambivalence to hostility. This was partly to do with the fact that I had seen her private things and places within the house and partly to do with her husband.

Her husband in that life was her now-partner and soul-love. He seemed to be away a lot but when he was around he was very pleasant and attentive to me. As I seemed to have had a genuinely cheerful disposition in that incarnation, I was nice to him. I do not think that Ruth liked this one bit as she had very clear cut ideas about social class deliniations which I had once violated by invading her space and was then crossing by being friendly to her husband, my 'superior.'

In the dream I witnessed my life in the kitchens where poor sight made me more clumsy and inept than I had been before. I was no more adept at the practicalities of life than I am now, as ever a soul more prone to daydreaming than looking where they are putting their feet! I also recalled how my relationship with Ruth's husband had turned more confiding and close as she appeared to have become more agitated and demanding. She constantly criticised both me and her husband and that could have been our common bond. In the dream I recall a silly infatuation with the husband which was probably more to do with him being Ruth's husband as I admired her still. I appeared to feel a non-sexual sort of 'crush' for the Ruth character and there was certainly no feeling of lust between me and the husband. There was a bond of 'being in the same boat' of living under Ruth's thumb and that made us closer than master and servant. He became enamoured of my simple charm and clumsy guile compared to his wife's haranguing and crotchety personality (which I believe to be due to her concealed ill-health rather than a genuine bad-humour.) He would flirt with me and try to kiss me and promise me that he would be with me...one day. It was all perfectly ineffectual and meaningless. Yet it was enough to push the Ruth persona into an act of pure spite and malice.

I recalled in this vivid dream-memory that I had been grabbed by a hired man as I went down the kitchen stairs one afternoon. As my sight was then none too special I do not know who he was except my soul-intuition that told me that Ruth had arranged this to happen. I was then bundled into a side room and there I died by some manner of means. It must have been mercifully quick as I had no memory of it at all except for my being suddenly dead. There was no residual sense of anger or malice on my part towards Ruth. All I carried over was a feeling of awe and a new sense of fear of her. The dream ended with my death although I have no clue how the hired man killed me.

I related this dream to Martin the following day. I was a little embarrassed to reveal a past-life crush on both Ruth and her soul-partner! Martin, calm and understanding as he was, listened to the tale and then told me to describe how I saw Ruth in that life. As an artist, I was able to draw the woman I saw as Ruth. She had looked quite similar to her current guise as souls often choose to do if they feel a particular pull or empathy to one of the 'characters' they have been before.

Just as Martin looked a lot like his previous Irish incarnation, Michael (this similarity in incarnate guise was what initially prompted my recognition of him. Clearly the same could be applied to my recognition of Ruth).

Martin observed my sketch of the Ruth that had been. He then said he would show me something to validate all I had seen in trance and in dream.

He took me to Waterstones bookshop in Bath city centre. There he pulled a book from the shelf in the poetry section. It was a volume by a woman author and there was a portrait of her on the front of the book. It was a portrait because this woman had lived in the age before photography. It was Ruth as she had been.

Ruth, it turns out, had known for many years that she was the reincarnation of this lady poet who had lived a fine life in England with her husband, a titled man who often went to war. When Ruth had been married to Martin she too had remembered a life in that same big house and had described to him its layout and contents, just as I had independently. The fact that Ruth had once been this poetess, as was so clearly displayed by the portrait on the cover of the book, explained to some degree my exaggerated awe and wonder of her. Not only was she rich and classy but she was also talented and acknowledged as a writer! I had been Ruth's servant in that life, I had 'seen' her. It was my 'truth' as far as truth be known.

Such moments of validation of what could be mere abstract imaginings, instead of past-life memories, are wonderful. I have had so many of them that I cannot help but be convinced of the belief in many lives as a personal truth. Still, it is always so special to actually see proof of your memories. Such a piece of evidence as the one Martin displayed to me cannot always be found as not everyone was famous in another existence. Most of us are the servants and labourers. In this instance the validation was clear due to the fame of some other soul that was involved.

What of this bizarre connection in terms of energies? Why had I met both Ruth and her man separately from Martin and still we had all managed to come together? I can only guess that the fates must balance such a large debt as my being killed deliberately at Ruth's bidding. She had to meet me again in order to put things right. How to do this? Well, it made sense that she should have married my soul-partner only for him to divorce her and come back to me. She did not really 'lose' or suffer in this manner as she too had met her own soul-love and could go to him. But the energies of the situation...her giving something to me that I wanted...fitted very well. Not only did I get to unite with Martin but I also cleared up my past-life trauma with Ruth.

I did not feel too traumatised by the whole affair compared to being burned alive or tortured it was an absolute doddle of an incarnation, but still Ruth was indebted to me and so the debt had to be worked out. One cannot gratuitously take a life and not give back something in return at a later date.

Imagine the scale on which these soul manoeuvres take place! Just contemplate what it takes for all of the souls involved in that scenario to be brought back together to conclude the interplay of energies appropriately. In this case, it helped that we two were with our soul-partners and so that connection helped our linking. Yet, if one considers that all the souls involved have their own agendas and their own webs of other soul-connections radiating out from them, other souls that need to see us for whatever reasons, how extraordinary it is that we should all meet up in such a way! How massive and complex the webs of possibility and probability must be! But ultimately, how fair.

We can never escape our fates and our soul-duties in the end. All is energy. Energy never dies, it transforms and moves on but it cannot be dissipated. We must be responsible for our soul actions and be prepared to pay accordingly to other souls for wrong doings. By this I do not mean for every time you do someone a minor injustice one must meet them again to recompense for it. Treading on somebody's toe does not require another lifetimes meeting! However, such things as murder do require atonement and a new understanding of energies in order for a harmonious conclusion to be reached. Further psychic investigation using the tool of guided meditation (as opposed to hypnosis) has revealed a long line of incarnations during which I was Ruth's social inferior or slave. The root incarnation was one in which I was one of twelve devotees of her Goddess cult in the ancient middle East. We all lead a calm and privileged life in an idyllic oasis, a walled temple with lush artificial gardens and a sacred pool.

Typically, my soul did not like the walled aspect of this setting, nor the way of being a devotee rather than an individual! My character in those times decided to go 'walk-about' outside of the temple boundaries during the daytime. This was strictly forbidden, we were only allowed into the temple grounds at night and were never allowed outside the gates at all. This was too much for my wild-soul to tolerate and I had to go into the 'real world' during daylight hours. There I delighted in watching the brightly coloured world of the traders. However, foolishly whilst I lurked around trying to look inconspicuous, I gained a suntan on my exposed parts. This somewhat gave me away on my return to base! A suntan was considered to be unclean and unholy in the eyes of our society and especially for one of the twelve virgins of this obscure moon-cult.

As a result of my dalliance I was cast out of the cosy confines of the temple into the world I had so wished to see. My destiny there was to be no more than a prostitute, a dancer for money in the street. My suntan and my outcast status brought me no respect and I was marked as a shamed woman. From then on I was free but life was hard. To have no respect from anyone is a severe punishment.

The energies from this first encounter with Ruth's soul were that I was annoyed with myself and somewhat ashamed for having let her cult down (my soul felt indebted to hers). Also, she was annoyed with me and embarrassed by my disobedience (her soul wished for obedience and penance from mine). The energies of mistress/slave or better/lesser, sinner/saint, dominant/submissive had been set up. It is these energies that are important in essence...not the stories or the characters although they help to put flesh on the bones of the message I am communicating here.

Now my link with Ruth is resolved and understood there is no further need for us to meet or communicate. We can move on and probably never meet again, we are not linked by anything but that one set of energies which began centuries ago. I am very glad that I understand that memories do not surface unless they have some relevance to current situations. That is why I had not recollected Ruth's incarnation with me until I met Ruth, although obviously I recognised her. Memories cannot surface constantly. What point in incarnating if all we ever get are memories of other lives? The memories do not occur to clutter up our present day lessons and life-tasks. They arise from the soul when the soul deems it appropriate that we should remember.

We meet up with those souls that we need to when it is appropriate for us to work with those energies involved. Had I met Ruth when I was seventeen it would have been a waste of soul-time. I couldn't have understood what was going on then and would have probably been frightened by the whole thing. If that would have happened then Ruth and I would have had to have met yet again in another life in the future and that would have involved all of the same complicated re-meeting of souls and all the altering of the webs that goes with it.

Would it have mattered if the memory had not been proved 'real?' Would it not have been relevant that my psyche deemed it important to tell me this story and therefore something about myself? The healing power of my unconscious mind is what matters, not a rock-solid belief in reincarnation. To know is to understand fully that I do not know. Whatever the ultimate truth, the important thing is to understand the lesson involved. The means by which the lesson is taught is largely irrelevant.

Although this example is a personal one, I feel that it adequately illustrates the soul-to-soul dilemmas and connections that we all have. They can be beautiful or terrible and we can find that we have been the recipient of wrong-doing or indeed, the wrong-doer. The energies can be subtle or brutal but they are always at work and always there. None of us can opt out of the game and we are all responsible, ultimately, for everything. Getting on one's moral high-horse, looking down on others or being violent or abusive to them - these are all attitudes and acts that will affect us all eventually.

We cannot ever claim that we are souls on a path to perfection, evolving into some ascended supreme white master. We are surely incorrect to perceive the universe from this Eurocentric, patriarchal and materially comfortable standpoint. That is simply tempting the fates to let us incarnate next time round as a cannibalistic female hunter on the other side of the world! We are more than male or female, more than our Western Ego-selves, more than a single isolated 'chosen' person on an elevated path to enlightenment. We are soul. Soul can be, and will be, anything it chooses to get a lesson or a point across. Manipulator can become manipulated, abuser the abused. Soul has no innate snobbery or prejudice. To illustrate this last point allow me to use another personal example relating to the Ruth scenario and the Ruth-related energy exchange that my soul became embroiled in over various lifetimes.

In the first instance, the Ruth-character was unimportant to me. The initial time I encountered her soul, she was Priestess in the Goddess-centred Eastern temple I previously described. It was only when our souls locked into each other by feeling personally aggrieved on an emotional level that we became important to each other. Then our incarnate guises were irrelevant but the playing out of the cosmic battle of wills was essential, rather as was illustrated in the centuries long enmeshment of the souls of Belinda, Nancy and the brother/husband figure (chapter four). The pattern of the soul-struggle usually followed the same dynamic for lifetime after lifetime, in my case servant to a mistress figure who I was in awe of. However, during a recent 'rounding up' meditation in which I tried to clear away any last vestiges of my connection to Ruth, a 'rogue' life surfaced.

In this life, be it real or a soul-drama which I concocted to fill a need, I was a man, a poacher, gypsy thief and, horrendous as it is to confess it, a rapist. The woman I habitually tormented and abused was Ruth in yet another form. This time it was she who was in my power, in thrall of me, that link still strong but in reverse. Ruth was, for once, the one in the pattern to feel that compulsion to obey and to serve, no matter how horrible things became between us. In that life, to my soul- shame I mercilessly abused that woman physically and mentally, leaving her with an illegitimate child in an age when that was frowned upon. The shame brought upon her by this child-bearing out of wedlock so eloquently reflected my own shame at being sunburned and ostracised in the Middle Eastern life. I, metaphorically speaking, disappeared off for a beer after mistreating that woman without a care in the world. The unpleasant but enduring image of 'me' in that life was my striding back into the woods, wiping my hands upon my trousers, whistling as I went having just brutalised the Ruth-character in her own home.

That rogue life was quite out of character for my soul and so perhaps I would like it to have been a symbolic vision of my soul rebelling against the Ruth-energies of domination and my response of being sublimated. I would very much like to believe that my soul would be incapable of such behaviours. Yet the soul will use any means to get a message across.

If we look at our lives incarnate as all happening at once rather than their being strung out behind us in succession in linear time, then it could be said that I am both rapist and raped all at once. My accessing the poacher/rapist memory now immediately connects me to lives were I have been raped, or beaten, or tormented, or murdered.

What do I learn from those experiences? I learn to forgive myself as that poacher/rapist. I feel the fear of the raped and the fear of the rapist - one and the same. I know with renewed perspective that there is no need for my soul to feel that fear anymore. I can accept that in the cycle of time I may step into any moment, any 'life' as if it were 'the now' and actively heal the soul with understanding. I observe the benefits of my own nature as a natural psychic which gives me 'instant access' to all of these aspects of self and my connection to others/the All. Most of all, I feel unconditional love for all the people that I have been and all those that are now and are yet to come. I am servant and rapist and mid-wife and rebellious noble-woman at this time in different spaces as well as being the Poppy Palin who learns from them all. I am the soul that weaves the web that is already spun...that of all lives to come. We are all The Weaver.

It is well to recall that we are all in 'costume' and are all 'wearing' bodies. We are soul, and there is nothing more liberating, humbling and levelling than that one truth. How can we not respect all with this knowledge?

We meet our potential selves everyday, in everyone. Be kind to the mistakes of others, learn from them and so heal your self - past, present, future.

Chapter Six

The Craft of the Wild

To be a Wildwitch one must essentially have a free spirit. This does not mean that one must suddenly take to a nomadic existence or live in a bender in a field! That sort of life, although entirely admirable as 'Green and Pagan', is not for everyone, just as Wildwitchery is not for everyone. The freedom I refer to is about individual freedom to choose, to decide by ones own code of morality and integrity. To make informed life choices on a spiritual basis, having a spirituality which is a living, growing part of us. Therefore our beliefs and our personal truths may evolve and change whilst our essential spiritual core of self, who we be, stands eternal. Eternal yet still evolving for the law of life is ceaseless change. Evolving, yet not into something 'perfect' but evolving in order to Be more harmoniously.

We may be Wildwitches whilst living in a tower block in Hackney or on a council estate in Manchester. We may have been born into a modern family with no interest in the Old Ways or perhaps we do not even have a clue who our biological parents are. We may know no other person who is inherently spiritual or we may be deliberately placed with those who are not. Our location, heritage or ancestry matters not one jot if we are born naturally psychic. If we have the sensitive ears to 'hear' and the spiritual eyes to 'see' we can be anywhere and still be effective Wildwitches.

Why? Because we have the opportunity to function more fully by being plugged into the grid of universal energies. This is achieved via a healthy relationship with our spiritual mentor, the Guide, who effectively acts as a wire to connect us to the power supply of the All. Through our natural ability to experience other Levels of Being we can work with the Otherworlds no matter what our material circumstances may be.

As we have seen in other chapters, magic and healing can be performed by pure thought and focussed intent without our having to have seen a hedgerow or an altar cloth! Wildwitchery is not the same as rural, traditional, ceremonial or hereditary Wicca or Witchery. Wildwitchiness is innate...a soul trait. It cannot be learned or taught but it can be developed in those in whom it lies dormant. This book has but encouraged the reader to Become, to rejoice in a way of Being, to wake the sleeping Wildwitch.

It is a joy to be such a Witch in an age when the worst one can expect is abuse with words which can hurt but not kill or maim as in past ages. We are free to think and act and be as we please within the boundaries of our society and the moral guideline of 'if it harm none'. We can rejoice in our way and meet others on parallel paths openly and without shame.

However, there is still something which keeps the majority of us quiet, something which subdues us and makes us hesitant to share our spiritual being with even close friends or family. Why? Are we really embarrassed about our beliefs and therefore our own selves? As with my labelling myself a Wisewoman out of a desire to be accepted, do we secretly wish to be seen as normal and not 'kooky'? Or are we still genuinely afraid?

In my own view, as I have stated in this book, to be a natural born psychic person, a Wildwitch, is just as normal, as real and as wholly acceptable as being a born musician, a born athlete or a born mechanic. Some things are inherent talents and we are encouraged to use these personal skills to earn our wage. Talents for painting or designing or riding or mathematics would all be considered gifts to be worked on and then cultivated into career options in the world. Our gifts are part of how we present ourselves to others, they distinguish us as individual souls and we are generally proud of these elements of Self.

With our wild spirituality and psychism we tend to hide our 'glow', to become unplugged from the Source. Our light remains firmly hidden under the proverbial bushel. For some reason unique to all possible gifts, our psychic talent is considered a negative. It is at best a sham or trick and at worst a kind of madness that may be contagious. By our own refusal to talk about it we support this ignorant, damaging assumption.

I can anticipate that the reader may respond to this suggestion by saying that people will not speak as they are tired of being misrepresented by the media and by other figures in society. I do accept that the media-driven world is still hungry for a silly story to further discredit the realm of magic, mysteries and the occult. Witchery has always come in for particular attention and derision or else flagrant sensationalism. Similarly psychism is regularly being 'disproven' or revealed as a fraudulent activity.

I myself was interviewed by a national daily newspaper, not a tabloid incidentally, who decided to falsify the entire report and make me into a freak. They invented a scenario whereby I had to dwell miles from anywhere in a caravan due to my apparent predisposition to making any electrical appliance go haywire if I came within spitting distance of it! This was a ludicrous nonsense and would have been laughable had it not made me appear an idiot in the public eye. Some may say it serves me right for courting publicity, after all, what can I expect? Why not just keep the old head down and keep quiet?

I did indeed consider never speaking to anyone about my gifts again, especially as I was given the 'I told you so' treatment by my then partner Martin (who had previously been accused falsely of ritual abuse by the press for declaring himself a practicing Witch.) However, my motivation for being interviewed then still stands, as does my purpose for writing books. There is a need for us to keep trying to gain understanding. Not to be accepted as normal or to be feted and congratulated but for those who feel alone with gifts they do not understand. In order for these people to feel comforted and to gain further understanding then we need to publically speak out.

We may need to do this over and over and get ridiculed many times in the process but like the Fool we must keep on getting up and stepping gladly into the abyss. If not then we risk those talented psychics who need guidance and encouragement and inspiration turning into people who are twisted by fear of themselves. Like an inherently superb musician who has been handed a violin but not instructed on the first rudiments of theory or practice, we leave isolated people alone with gifts they cannot hope to gain a grip without support and information.

How much more damaging to the untrained psychic individual to leave them with the Otherworlds hammering on their psyche for attention than to leave a gifted musician alone with a violin they are untrained to play? Not only do we allow the lone psychic to flounder with untapped energies at large but we keep those who are in contact with them in a state of ignorance. If articles and conversations on Witchery and the Craft of the natural psychic were as plentiful and as regular as those on sport, cooking or childcare then we would have both a healthier and more fulfiled group of people. Those who knew of sensitive Witches in the family or at work could not only allow them to talk openly about their doings but could also benefit by getting guidance and spiritual healing from the psychic. The psychic in turn is going to be nourished as a whole individual, not in denial of any aspect of self, and so will do more good ultimately in terms of Otherworldly contact and interaction.

I have indeed witnessed a perfectly acceptable Pagan magical Coven infiltrated by reporters and brought down to the lowest common level. This was achieved as the Coven members, being human, fell into the trap of being flattered and ego-massaged by the cunning infiltrators. But it was deemed a valid thing to do in the first place as we (almost) all buy newspapers which exploit and use sensationalism as a selling point. Somewhere along the line we can take responsibility for the fact that we demand to be entertained by other's misfortunes, the more lurid and revealing the better.

I do not for one moment believe that the Coven was infiltrated and made to look silly by Christian activists or any other set of religious persons with a moral axe to grind. The Coven was discredited as a means of entertaining a readership, a readership who already half-believed that Witchcraft was a farcical fantasy indulged in by perverts or wierdoes. The main aspect of exploitation was, not surprisingly, the sex element of ritual and magic within such a group. The whole debacle was a result of a none to subtle blend of pride and preening mixed with fulfilling a public need for sleaze and sordid detail.

Nobody is innocent here and it would be simply paranoia to read anything more such as a modern Witch hunt into the situation. It was yet another case off making fools out of those who are different, this time to provide titilation for a gossip-hungry populace. It also continued the process of making the unexplained and hidden into a crude joke of the basest level. The press, generally, have no intention of spreading enlightenment when they can provoke more discord and mis-understanding, which in turn provides more in the way of a desirable storyline. Understanding and harmony do not make for good copy. It is as simple (and as dumb) as that! Hands up who has ever bought a newspaper more than once which indulges in such behaviours? So it goes on.

Maybe our true occult knowledge and ability is beyond 'their' comprehension and we make them feel inadequate?! Whatever, to use this one instance of media exploitation as a case of the Christians getting the stakes ready is purely sowing further seeds of division and derision between spiritual groups. Obviously, any such ridicule of an occult matter causes personal and group distress, disempowers both individually and collectively and causes all sorts of in-fighting and accusations within the occult 'community' (known popularly as Bitchcraft). Certainly, the Pagan Federation, a voluntary body which works for promoting positive under-standing across all spiritual paths, would say that there are many cases of defamation of Witches and other practitioners. I would never dispute the damage that such crude and ignorant displays in the press (or otherwise) can cause. I have been a victim of this on more than one occasion and it takes some getting over to know that your sensitive and sensible interview has been warped and misquoted to represent you as a harmless nutter at best, a dangerous dabbling psychopath at worst.

To blame this disharmony on Christians is wrong and to consequently use fear of Christian persecution as an excuse for remaining silent is inappropriate. As we may have come to appreciate, we may have had Christian lives ourselves, other incarnations wearing a Christian mask for the sake of our soul's spiritual quest. We may understand that those who choose to walk in ignorance and fear wear many other guises other than purely Christian ones. The main 'culprit' is society and society contains me and you. Ignorance can be dispelled from within if we start looking beyond masks and 'enemies' and start concentrating on the energies involved instead.

This derision from society would never stop me from speaking again and again until it comes right. This is not due to a need in me to blow my own egotistical trumpet, nor because I like the sound of my own voice. It is because of a woman that I shall refer to as J.

J represents many other silent figures across the country, locked into a destructive cycle because of the suppression of their natural Witch selves. I used to be one such figure, and I see my young self in J. I was introduced to her by Robert who knew nothing of the tormented nights she had spent for years due to her psychic ability going unchecked. J liked to appear 'normal'. Yet J was a woman in a state of near collapse on all levels.

Like myself before her, J had grown quite adept at hiding the torment of such isolation. She was unable to sleep alone as she was disturbed by voices, visions and presences untold who she couldn't 'switch off'. She had never dared tell a soul and had never met anyone who could shed some light on the problem. She felt singularly cursed. By day she held down a civil service job, she owned her own house and had a partner who remained oblivious to her torment. She had tried to split from this man as she felt that he could not understand her predicament in a million years, She felt all the more lonely trapped with a man who had no idea that she was in spiritual and emotional pain. She would not remove the man entirely from her life as she considered it too much to be alone with her psychic disturbances every night.

The seemingly constant flow of waking dreams, visions, voices and feelings that invaded her space made J truly terrified. Not only terrified but out of control. She knew that she was not insane but that this terrible isolation with her psychic mayhem would maybe make her so. When I met J I saw no hint of this despair as she had put a tight lid on it and was attempting to struggle on.

144

On about our fourth meeting we were talking about her house which is beautifully decorated . She admitted that she got no pleasure from it and hinted that she had trouble sleeping. Intuitively I began to reveal to her my own night problems with restless spirits and human 'thought forms' which were attracted to me like iron filings to a magnet. As was the case with J, I had witnessed most of my psychic intrusions at night when the rest of the western world has stopped thinking and sending out its own transmissions.

At night, the 'airwaves' of humanity are less cluttered with all day-to-day exchanges and so the spirit realm and the lower astral are more able to come through and be noticed. We tend to be in bed when these things occur, in a space of quiet reflection which allows us to pick up any vibration or sound more acutely. In the case of the nuisance 'thought forms', humanity's 'psychic trash', they can positively thrive on causing distress and alarm. Night is a better time to chose to 'haunt' someone, especially if it is a thought form which uses fear as a kind of fuel to grow and sustain its existence. When we are alone in the dark we are far more susceptible to fear and anxiety than if we were bothered by a disembodied voice in the supermarket or in a sunny garden. Not only can they transmit clearer at night but we receive more acutely and we then do them the favour of feeding their need for fear - it makes them feel more important and inflates their form.

In the case of genuine human souls who have passed over then it may be that the only time they can attract our attention adequately is when we are finally lying still and quiet in bed. I myself used to dread bedtime and insomnia was a regular complaint. If I was not troubled by past life dreams of a disturbing nature then it was voices or noises in an empty room. At night we cannot put extraneous sounds down to neighbours or the television in another room. I used to be in a state of panic through the small hours, helplessly witnessing yet another intrusive presence, some curious, some downright invasive and unpleasant. It only ceased to bother me when I learned I could give it the astral two fingered salute and that I could protect myself. I could, and did, regain control and although I am regularly bothered by 'visitors' I know how to banish them and make sure my space is protected against further invasion. 1 advised J. that I could teach her these methods and that she could regain control also.

I took a risk in revealing my true way to J as she could have turfed me out of her house there and then and I could have immediately lost her friendship. I had revealed to her that I was a psychic and Witch and in so doing I had run the risk frightening her still further. As I have no need of a friend from whom I must conceal my true self then I simply had to take a chance and hope she could relate to what I said. As it was I had intuited her disturbance correctly as she seized upon this information and began begging me to tell her how to deal with it. The problem was, how does one woman help another in the space of a social visit with a subject as deep and multi-layered as the Otherworlds and the psychic arts?

I could advise her to read my book, other works on psychic protection and introductions to the Craft in its various aspects and esoteric traditions. Yet what she needed was to talk. She needed to be seen as normal and to hear another fully functioning, sane adult tell her that it was okay and she was not alone. Moreover, there was something that she could do about it. I could immediately give her the rudiments of psychic safety, the visualisation of the protective suit, the astral safe place to retreat to and the pathways into meeting her Guide.

How to remove her ingrained fear of the unknown? How to inspire her to feel good about her gift and to positively use it? How to make her appreciate that not all the voices in her ear were nuisance callers? I could attempt all this, over time, but for the time being I explained to J that she was a psychic too.

That her soul acted as a bright astral flame to which spirits and thought forms were attracted. This seemed as good a way to synopsis it as any. I said that this was a positive thing to imagine herself shining so brightly that other beings were attracted to her, that she was like a beacon that the disembodied used to home in on. From this I could point out that those human souls that she attracted would not wish to harm her and would wish to speak to her and also through her in a variety of ways. I endeavoured to stress the positive aspects for J. saying that this was a great privilege to act as a go-between twixt the worlds, to bring comfort to relatives and friends of the deceased. As for the other 'flotsam', she was delighted that she could have the power to tell them where to go. The basic method I suggested to J. for dealing with intrusion is as follows:-

Suggestion for working with psychic intrusion

Firstly, relax, close the eyes and open the third/mind's eye. You may imagine yourself standing in a dark place to begin with. If one has established a 'safe' meditation place, go there.

1. Find a symbol which appeals to you which can act as your protective symbol. For myself, I use two. Firstly, I visualise (in their minds eye) a large silver pentagram (five pointed star within a circle). Not only do I like the shape and find it aesthetically pleasing (which is important) but it has esoteric meaning in tradition. The five points are the four elements plus a fifth which they are born of - the All (ether, the void, the womb). The circle is the circle between the worlds that we can create to work with the All, the elements can be called on to protect us as we work there. There are many variations on this understanding but this is my own simple basis for choosing the pentagram. It is, obviously, not just some fancy gee-gaw for wearing on a ring or necklace! Choose a symbol for its resonance with your aesthetic eye by all means but do

research its origin to discover what power you are evoking. All such symbols of antiquity, the spiral labyrinth, the ankh, the OM, a rune etc all have vibrations and resonances which cannot be ignored.

Spend time choosing a symbol. Imagine it so big that you may pass it over your head and down your body. If this is a circular symbol, all the better as it can be seen as hoop passing over the head and down. Any other symbol made large enough can be held by its sides and the same process followed. When it is at your feet you are standing inside the symbol and it begins to glow. You are standing in the silver glowing symbol of choice, feel its particular power and energies and relax. The glow fades but the symbol is now burned into the place where you 'see' yourself standing.

You may now take further smaller silver symbols and place them about your person. I usually place one upon my mind's eye, (third eye, between the two physical eyes and slightly above on the brow.) With the basic guideline that the third eye is about psychic vision/clarity, throat for communication, heart for emotion, stomach for intuition/gut feeling and personal creativity and genitals for energy/health (with the area to the crown governing the entire whole self) then one can make an informed decision as to which area of the etheric body may need most coverage. This would be relevant if one thought there was a psychic intrusion or attack which was playing on one of these vulnerable areas, manifesting in an illness perhaps. Or alternatively if one wished for particular guidance which would mean opening up on an intuitive or emotional level.

A second symbol can be given at a later date by the Guide. This will be given if you ask for it, or if the Guide finds you to be in need of a powerful personal talisman at that time. This symbol may be 'universal' as in the first chosen symbol, or it may be obscure and have a meaning which is strictly understood by you and the Guide on a soul- level. I will not disclose my own as it is wisdom not to reveal the personal symbol. This may be used in the same way as the universal symbol and will be understood thus. All astral 'traffic' will pay heed to either symbol, not only because it has ancient and ingrained power which resonates but because you give it that status and belief. In the astral realm, you can have this status and can create your rules in your space.

2. Having stood inside the symbol(s) and having perhaps used others about the astral self, then imagine a protective suit upon the astral body which covers all, but all, parts. With this in mind, desiring an image of a suit which has to protect real bodies in 'hostile' or alien places, I now 'see' my astral self in a space suit! Not very cosmic or romantic but highly effective! The silver suit (of any description, in this case the padded suit, boots, gloves and bubble helmet of a space traveller) are donned in the imagination. It would be effective if one could visualise the astral self entirely covered in tin foil like an Egyptian mummy's bandages, save for a pair of wrap around silver shades perhaps! Anything goes as long as it is silver (reflects away any unwanted astral debris that has an attempt at penetrating the psychic armour, like a cosmic mirror) and covers all of your 'imaginary' (but very real) astral self.

3. Either chosen symbol may be used to create a sacred space on the ground. Visualise the symbol glowing and call anyone you may have need to speak to into this space. By your astral 'law' they are then held there and may cause no harm. This does not mean you are free to boss them about when they enter your space. Guests into astral space must be treated with respect, integrity, honesty and kindness no matter how foul or rude they may be.

The symbol is vital in protecting the astral traveller. Think of it as the equivalent of psychic mosquito repellent!

N.B. given the flexibility of the Wildwitch, this symbol can be altered at any time as it is grown out of or if it no longer feels suitable. This is not to be done on a whim as one may change socks!

4. There are two options now. If it is simply an undisturbed night's sleep that you require then holding the image of yourself fully protected in your gear whilst standing in your symbol will be adequate. One can supplement this by using the personal or universal symbol as a shield. Holding this up before you, imagine it glowing and make it clear that no psychic intrusion may enter your space as you sleep. This can be done also by imagining that you hold up a mirror. This is a good way of making sure that you will be untroubled at night. However, it only lasts for that night and will need to be repeated every night. It is really only a temporary measure if one is being seriously 'hassled' by the other side. Saying that, if it is done regularly enough then it will deter even the most persistent of thought-forms or intruders of a lower level. They will soon get tired of being around one who can protect themselves against their annoyances,. They have no fun if we simply reflect all their stupidity and nastiness back at them, night after night and they will soon move on or hopefully cease to be altogether.

5. If one really feels either the need to banish a particularly troublesome thought form (and they can indeed be both big and unpleasant in the extreme) then further action must be taken. Similarly, if one believes that the intrusion comes from a genuine psychic 'caller' with a message, a human spirit or other soul figure, then a method such as this will also help.

The Guide is essential to this process. If one is in dire straits and needs psychic protection immediately, yet has not the experience of mediating with a Guide and a safe place then simply calling on the Guide at this point will be adequate. The Guide may be called by either a) imagining your universal symbol on the ground nearby or b) imagining a circle of blue flame on the ground nearby, (cold blue protective flame, not a raging inferno) and calling upon the personal Guide with love and respect to appear to help you with the task in hand. You may not 'see' anyone specifically but be assured that they are there. Your Guide will come if you use correct forms of address and the right sort of attitude for calling on a valued and dear friend for help. Whether you know them or not, this is what they are to you. Their presence will be felt if not 'seen'.

If one does 'see' the Guide be sure to 'check them out'. This may be done by use of the pointing stick/mirror/stone method described earlier in chapter three. Use this method to check out anyone, but anyone, who appears in the astral space. No matter if the spirit who appears claims to be Great Aunt Mabel or no, check it out. Likewise check out the Guide each and every time that you attempt a psychic work. I recently omitted to check out my trusted Guide and was half way into a complicated journey on the astral when I realised what I had forgotten. I was then effectively travelling in unknown and potentially hazardous territory with a spirit who could have been the equivalent of an axe wielding maniac. I was lucky that time but it certainly shook me up and taught me a lesson.

After inviting the 'pest' into your astral space to step into the symbol you provide for it then you may talk to it or else simply ask for the Guide's help in sending it to the place in the universe where it may best receive healing. Then picturing a column of light coming down onto the symbol, 'see' the pest being taken (beamed up or down) to this appropriate place. It is not ours to know where this is. My advice is not to engage with the pest in a verbal exchange as this only further strengthens any link. It is probably adept at deception and will only confuse the issue with its antics. It does not wish to be banished. Banish it with love, offer it healing no matter how annoying it has been.

151

If the pest turns out to be a recognisable living human spirit - the astral body of some actual person... (check it out to make sure they are who they say they are!) then by all means talk to he or she and reason with them before sending them off to be healed. One may find that the astral pest is none other than a friend or neighbour! If the astral intruder is a deceased spirit who wishes to communicate then again do chat away before sending them off to be healed.

6. When the tasks are completed, and there may be more than one intruder to deal with in a session, then thank the Guide and ensure that the astral space is 'tidy' i.e. completely free of any residual spirit. The Guide will assist with this. It is vital to be courteous to the Guide, do not leave the astral level until you have expressed gratitude to them.

If J had discovered that night that she was able to up a guitar and instantly play along to records, or if she had, with the minimum of instruction been able to rewire her house herself then she would have been brimming with news and enthusiasm. Since she discovered that she is as sensitive as they come and has the potential to talk to those in spirit, to gain insights from the Otherworld and to help others by these means then she felt that it was somehow inappropriate to tell anyone. It was secret, weird, going to be misunderstood. This is why we do J a disservice and this is why we perpetuate the myths by remaining silent. Forget the press, misinformation and defamation, it is the lonely and the isolated who suffer.

What could, in reality, be more fantastic than being able to give someone a message from a departed loved one? J's gift is one of the finest, surely? Our abilities to converse with an unseen populace is remarkable, wonderful and cause for celebration.

If we consider what an absolute honour it is to have been born being able to see beyond the veil and hear across the realms then we could scarcely be worried about the sad few who still resort to name calling. We best educate those people by shining, with a genuine sense of self worth.

The only way to reach J or anyone like her is to communicate. Books are fine, great for back up. How much better to have a real human being who will honestly pass on the green cross code of psychism and be a reassurance and sounding board?

By speaking up we destroy stereotypes by proving our diversity, the fact that we could be anyone, from shop worker to computer analyst to vet. We have the intelligence to articulate sanely and with feeling. The feelings behind our sentiments are often missing from our books, the joy and the struggle both go flat on paper. We know the power of collective energies and still we choose to remain in pockets across the land, in couples or closely knit groups, or as solitary workers. The power that could link us lies dormant in denial, all because we may perhaps, only perhaps, meet a prejudice which calls us a few names.

We can only teach effectively and reach out adequately by being living examples. Not impossible icons but people who put Witch on their business card as they would do carpenter or biologist. It is not only who we be but it is what we do because we have a talent for it. I write this from an intense pride in those who can 'see' and 'know'. The Wise have been truly persecuted and no doubt have returned in this age when there is no torture, rape or execution to face. I consider the psychic ones, the Wildwitches, to be of a soul-race, widespread and dissipated in their collective energies. We have been soul-battered and our psyches bruised over the millennia in our countless incarnate guises. Yet now we are comparitively free. The only thing holding us back from being truly free is our own reluctance to share. We let each other down by our reticence and we weaken ourselves individually and collectively as a result.

So what of this Wildwitchery? What is the point of being a Wildwitch and a natural born psychic? It may produce the odd interesting story and a labyrinth of spiritual questions and conundrums but what is the core purpose and motivation?

I was reminded of my own purpose by J's mother Anna who came to me after hearing I was involved with her daughter. She realised my need to help the long suffering J and was interested in who I was to be so presumptuous as to think I had a solution. J had lent her my first book which she had found absorbing and not only did she now wish to encourage my work with J but she also wished to ask for help of her own.

The story of J's family is not a happy one. J's father took his own life when the child was an infant and her mother had been in a state of grief and shock since. She needed to know that her husband was somehow still in existence and that he was happier on some level. Anna asked me to try to contact her late husband and she presented me with a small photograph of him to guide me. I was initially struck, by looking at this photo, that this man would not wish to speak to me. However, I was obliged to go through the process to contact a spirit. The steps that I followed on this occasion were as follows:-

1.   Sitting comfortably in a room lit only by candle light I kept the photograph of the man I sought in front of me so that I might focus upon it as I went into trance.

2.   I opened the third eye and imagined pulling my pentagram of protection over my head until I was sitting within its glowing silver circle. I then drew a further circle of blue flame around myself as I sat. Searching for a soul in the Otherworlds can leave one very open indeed to all manner of pretenders and intruders. I imagined putting on my silver suit also, for ultimate personal protection.

3. I spent a considerable while going into a relaxed state whilst focussing upon the photo before me. The focus was not on the mans mortal appearance but rather I met his eyes in the photo and concentrated on locating his immortal self, the eyes being the window to the soul. I have recognised many people from past-life encounters merely from the eye contact. Physically there may be no similarity, their sex may have even changed, but the eyes cannot disguise what lies within.

4. Closing my physical eyes and keeping my minds eye open I then went to my astral safe place to find my Guide. This was done methodically and slowly as the task ahead was a hard one and I wished to imbue the whole scenario with as much realism and clarity as was possible. Thus I gave my familiar astral landscape as much attention as I could in the hope that the unfamiliar soul I would meet would be viewed with a heightened focus.

5. I called on my Guide, did the necessary checks to the Guide's authenticity, and asked them to take me to this man.

6. I was taken to an appropriate astral location for a meeting to take place. At this point I was prepared to be given guidance by verbal means or symbolic imagery. I am also prepared to take a message 'through me' by means of 'automatic' (spirit guided) writings - channelled writing. It is vital to ensure the spirit is who they say they are before allowing this process.   .

7. Guidance was given, thanks were offered and I was escorted back.

As it happened, it was not Anna's deceased husband who wished to talk. Anna's Father (J's Grandfather), also in spirit, came through instead and explained to me the predicament of her late husband's soul. It appeared that the man had loved Anna and her family so much that to link with them as a Guide or spirit contact at that point would have re-opened old wounds. As he had taken his own life he was going through a process of soul healing. He was not in disgrace nor was he being punished. Other souls who loved him were ensuring he healed those terrible wounds of soul trauma from such an unnatural and painful passing. The man was no longer angry but regretted the loss of his family very deeply. He felt sadness but no personal blame.

Anna's father gave me the message that the man was waiting for his family to join him and that in the meantime he would be going through this process of soul-therapy. Anna's father expressed the difference in time scales as we in the manifest experience them compared to how he and the late husband experienced them. He stated that the husband would not be waiting for earth-years in order to see his family again. He explained that in the Other Realms there was an ability to 'switch off' and float in a timeless state, that time was irrelevant and that a soul was able to float, suspended for immeasurable periods gaining healing. This seems rather like sleep for the soul.

The father claimed that the husband was taking time to float out of time and place and was simply 'being'. Any actual contact between he and his bereaved wife would be detri=mental to this mending of his eternal Self. A suicide is like a soul-earthquake and it needs a lot of love to even begin to mend the rifts. I myself had a friend who committed suicide and I could never 'contact' him, it was as if he had vanished astrally. Now I understand a little more of why he was 'unavailable'. It is hard for the people that suicides leave behind as they are the very ones we want to contact psychically to see if they are alright now and no longer in pain or troubled. Also to clear up any lingering earthly problem we had with the deceased soul which may or may not have been a contributing factor to their untimely demise.

From this encounter, I learned that we may need to let go and allow the capable guardians of this soul in the Otherworlds to heal and mend. I am assured that this process is the reason why a soul is 'incommunicado'. No soul ever ceases to be, suicides do not get refused access to the Otherworlds.

Anna's father appeared in vivid technicolour and in full Earthly guise to me. He was extremely keen to prove who he was and kept showing me what he wore and what he did when he was alive last time around. He pointed out various quirks and personal things which would help Anna know that he was indeed who he said he was and that the guidance about her husband was genuine. Of course, I 'checked the man out' also. He was a charming and animated character who spoke to me in images as well as words. This can be a little confusing as I then have to put my own interpretation on the image to some degree. I believe that the soul may show me images as 'in spirit' they do not need to rely solely on words as we do.

He did actually also tell me things 'verbally'. This clear verbalising and his very definite appearance as the man he had been helped me describe him accurately to Anna later on. I was not only able to describe his last incarnate self to her but I could relay the messages he had given to me in his own language using his own patterns of speech and nuances. This brought the character to life and made it more rounded and 'believable' to the recipient of the messages (Anna). As the spirit of her father had allowed me to channel his writings I was able to remember and recall far more of our astral 'conversation'. Some discarnate souls love to do this, it gives them a chance to present a lengthy discourse on 'the other side' and can be absolutely fascinating. The soul usually is just as fascinated with the nature of the Otherworlds and having a bigger picture on the meaning of life! There is also a sense of great pleasure in being able to have an actual conversation again; there is a sense of their missing being manifestly 'in body' and so they enjoy the experience of being able to chat as they used to.

As a channelled writing is not a two way conversation (but it can be given as a response to a question to the soul you have contacted) the soul can tend to waffle on and on about the new existence they have and their philosophies! This is wonderful to a point but it is certainly a good idea to have up to three prepared questions to ask to keep the soul 'on track' and get some clarity! Anna's father was aware he was waffling and he edited himself! He was a truly amazing soul who understood the need to prove that he was genuinely the soul that he said he was (so he gave information only he would know). He also appeared clearly in his last form so that I could describe him to Anna and finally he gave valuable insights into the 'afterlife' which we could take seriously as he had already proved his 'validity'.

Anna was delighted at the description of her father and at the channelled writings which were given in his manner of talking with his turns of phrase and nuances. She was able to show me a photograph of her father taken not long before his passing and he was exactly as I had witnessed him on the astral level. Anna was, of course, saddened by her ex-husband's grief but heartened to know that he was still in existence and would be waiting to meet with her again upon her own passing.

Anna was so delighted with my gift that she was keen for me to move on and see other of her bereaved friends who would have welcomed my assistance. However, she insisted that I must charge an hourly rate. This troubled me as I was still firmly stuck in the Wisewoman's mode which did not consider money at all. I would sincerely like to complete all my exchanges of work by a barter system. I believe that every act of work we undertake for someone is a gift of our talent and energy and therefore there should be a receipt of energy from them to balance it up. It matters not if this energy is financial energy or the energy of an equal act of work. There must be an exchange. although I feel distinctly uneasy about joining the marketplace and selling my psychism I am aware that I too must survive in this age. I will accept barter gladly but I must also accept financial recompense for my efforts, within reason. Going back to my analogy of the psychic being as valuable as a plumber, well, a plumber would not work for free and psychic labour can be pretty intense, as well as very worthwhile. Mending a psychic 'burst pipe' of energies can be just as invaluable as fixing a water leak and equally as exhausting!

Part of my concern with charging for psychic help was "what if I can't help this time, what if it is beyond my means?" This does indeed happen. In the case of a friend, Ellen, she requested my intervention between her mother and her mother's abusive partner. I was concerned as the mother had not directly asked me herself but I suggested that I would be able to look at the astral implications of their scenario rather than going in and changing them. I could talk to the abusive partner astrally and see why he was behaving badly. At no time, under no circumstance, would I attempt to manipulate or change another soul astrally. Nor would I go poking around without an invitation of any sort. All I could do was to try to connect with the problem. The method that I employed for this task is similar to those used in other astral operations.

1. Protect the self using both symbol (to the necessary extent) and the silver protective suit.

2. Go to the astral safe place and call on the Guide.

3. Either draw a circle of fire /protective symbol on the ground and call the required soul/s into it or ask to be taken to a convenient astral location in order to meet them. In either case, keep a safe distance by placing yourself, the Guide and the soul/s that you seek in protective circles.

4. Follow all 'checking' procedures (this should have been done for the Guide, obviously).

5. Engage in any business with the soul. You cannot command them and they have had the courtesy to turn up for you to discuss pertinent matters with them. It would be folly to coerce, bully or threaten another soul. Find out how they feel and why they behave in the way that they do (discover a bigger picture, dispel ignorance). Reason with, rather than demand from, souls and explain they are causing harm by their actions. Discuss what may be done, avoid telling them.

6. Ask that the soul may be taken to the place in the universe appropriate to them where they would best receive healing. Thank them for their time and co-operation and thank the Guide also. Return to the manifest.

7. I could add here that a) one must ground the self after any astral encounter - eat, drink and feel the solid ground beneath you. This is an essential if you wish to avoid feeling 'spaced out' and 'disconnected' from the manifest.

b) One can ground better and recall more by immediately making notes of all that was seen and heard in a journal (a Witch's Book of Shadows and Light). You may think that you will recall everything on returning to the here and now. Be sure that you will not. Writing down our astral adventures is a good discipline.

It also helps bring insights and clarity to any symbology that we may encounter in guidance.

In Ellen's case I had no personal item/photo of the abusive partner to focus on (as with Anna's late husband). I had never met him and I had no clues as to his soul, save that he was obviously currently unhappy and disturbed. Consequently the images I received were fuzzy and ill-formed. The man appeared to me repeatedly as a large and angry child. His soul was in a state of angry flux and was incapable of relating to me as a fully functioning form. Instead he sent me images of a spoiled baby throwing its toys at me and appearing in dressing up costume in the circle of protection.

I managed to ascertain, after some considerable work and patience, that the man himself was in a state of resentment over a father who had never loved him for himself. He had only wanted this Fatherly approval, the opinions of women mattered little to him. I would imagine there was a series of past-life causes for this attitude, but I was unable to continue to pursue them as I did not have his permission. He did not wish me to help or to tell me anything except that he hated his Father for not approving of his less manual and practical, more cerebral skills.

He did tell me his profession and gave me the idea that his father had wished him to be better with a spanner than with numbers, as this was his forte as an office worker. It was all rather unpleasant and I even ended up having an astral spanner flung at me in frustration by this deeply unhappy soul. His antipathy towards himself reflected out to Ellen's mother and his lack of respect for women's views compounded this .

There was nothing that I could do for the situation. I received confirmation from Ellen of the man's profession and that there had indeed been an odd dynamic between father and son. I was sorry that I had managed to contact the right soul but that I had to report that on this occasion he had no desire to be helped or to work things through. I could see only destruction at the end of the line for the damaged and fraught soul which needed extensive healing. As the man is also an alcoholic, this may have blurred the contact further as I could not reach his true self. Three things may have been responsible for this apparent failure:-

1. Lack of manifest cooperation between myself as psychic and the couple themselves, an absence of personal connection. The couple were in ignorance of my involvement. I had been given no personal invitation by those directly involved to intervene between them.

2. Lack of a personal object to focus on in place of actual contact with the person/s involved.

3. Dealing with the soul of a manifest alcoholic - a soul probably surrounded by a cloud of thought-forms attracted by constant inebriated states. It would take me too long to work with them all and dispel them. Besides, I had no permission to do so.

I would be afraid of such a failure occurring in the arena of paid work as this work for Ellen was a favour for a friend. However, if I can get guidance as to why the contact is difficult, then I can work through the situation accordingly. I can also explain to the client why the psychic work was unsuccessful. One still has to pay a car mechanic for their time when they work on a car which cannot be fixed and has to be scrapped. The effort involved is recompensed. Still, this is a difficult area, the world of paying for guidance of a psychic nature. I believe that if one tries with all sincerity to avoid egotism, exploitation and greed and to act with integrity and wisdom then it is right and good to accept (reasonable) energy (money) for a psychic action.

The point of being a Wildwitch, then?

Not everyone is born this way. There would be no point in a teacher going to train for four years at university and then never entering a classroom, just staying at home to learn more from books. There would be no point in a plumber reading all the manuals and texts available but never doing a job. We must help people. We must help ourselves. The energies of such positive actions reflect back and out to the All. In being ourselves we do much good.

Therefore, in essence, the crux of being a natural born psychic, a Wildwitch, is to know thyself and act accordingly. All else follows.

Referring back to our age of 'instant' everything, we expect guidance to be of direct relevance to this day, this moment. Guidance will not span decades (how could it, with all the energies and interweavings that would involve? So much could change over such a long period in an astral sense!) Guidance may cover a period of months during which key changes or patterns will occur. Guidance may well predict those patterns given the path the individual is now on. It may offer alternative paths. It may give names of people not yet met. It may refer to spirits that the person is not physically aware of being present.

I recently did a piece of guidance for a stranger from whom I had only a photograph. For her I did some guided writing from her own Guide who talked to me in meditation. The woman did not have prior knowledge of her Guide or of a spirit that the Guide referred to as being a pest. It was all abstract to the woman! Abstract in the sense that she could believe in them but had no direct experience of them in a 'real' manner. Yet because she could understand how these things, these abstracts, were affecting her life then she could place some credence on the guidance! She could not see the spirit but she could appreciate how it may be affecting her life-choices.

This bit of guidance could have been received badly as maybe this woman wished for more concrete facts in the words I psychically received for her. She may have desired dates, days, the whys and wherefores of her life. She may have wished to know she was guided by Uncle James, who she knew had actually existed, rather than a nameless Indian.

Such expectation could have destroyed the subtler interpretation of the abstract energies which were truly affecting her manifest existence. After all, nobody wishes for guidance if they are well, happy and settled. Guidance is wished for if there are troubles to be cleared up. As exciting as it may be for the recipient to know their troubles would be over next Wednesday when a man called John would approach them in Marks and Spencers, guidance would be more likely to reveal that their troubles may be better understood if they accepted the disharmony that certain energies caused!

Not all guidance has to be 'not what the person wishes to hear', sometimes it is plainly not what that person can manifestly understand! Guidance deals with the patterns and energies of the Otherworlds and the spirit. It is not really there to tell us which bus to catch next Tuesday in order to meet the love of our life! It can, however, explain why you may be blocked against meeting that love.

Guidance is not prescriptive, it merely suggests or offers understanding. Due to its nature, guidance can always be spurned because it does not come up with great personal insights or information. Clairvoyants who theatrically proclaim that "you bought a new sofa yesterday" may elicit a gasp of "how could you have known that? Wow!" but they are usually employing the (clever) trick of mind-reading.

Guidance is not about invading a person's consciousness to pluck out thrilling 'nobody-else-could-have-possibly-known-that!' snippets. This kind of clairvoyance may be a hundred times more fascinating as everyone loves to hear about themselves. It may 'prove' that psychic communication is 'real'. It is entertaining and it is clever but it is ultimately self-serving. True guidance tells us what we don't know so that we may understand ourselves and the All with more harmonious results. This is often an uncomfortable process as I have amply illustrated elsewhere in this book. Growth is uncomfortable, perhaps whilst re-affirming what we think we already know is safe. Ultimately we must decide how we wish to be, there is no right or wrong in opting for the safe over the uncomfortable. A Wildwitch, however, has no choice in the matter. The only lesson here is to know thyself.

The purpose and meaning of Wildwitchery is to know the self and to act accordingly. All else follows from there. We can study all the manuals in the world and not help a single soul, nobody would find help from a plumber who was all theory and no practice! We are here to help, it is the role of our soul type. The energies of our positive endeavours reflect out and back to the All. Round and around. We do much good.

To conclude I have included three case scenarios, actual problems that I have faced and dealt with. I hope that they will give the reader further ideas and insights into the work of the natural psychic. This may be for the purpose of carrying out the work themselves or simply understanding and respecting it.

Case One. The Problem of a Negative Soul-Link (Past-Life)

Name: Mark

Relation to myself: The man who taught me how to tattoo with whom I sought an apprenticeship.

Nature of problem: I knew Mark in a previous life. In that other life he had been responsible for having my lover killed. He had pretended to be a friend to my lover but had been spying on him in order to turn him in to my powerful father.

Energies involved: Mark's soul wished to contact me again to make amends for his responsibility in killing my lover. As my lover then was my partner at that point in my current life, then Mark also wished to 'make up' with him. Mark himself was totally unaware of his soul's desire to make amends. Both my partner and I recognised the man psychically for who he was.

Any other factors: Mark was choosing to behave very badly towards me against his soul's wishes. He mis-used his power in the tattoo apprenticeship situation and was physically and verbally abusive. His energies were of greed, lust and pride. In company he felt the need to humiliate me whilst in private, alone in a teacher-pupil situation with me, he was polite and deferential.

Psychic diagnosis: The energies here conflicted, Mark's soul-will was to treat me well in apology for his past-life mis-demeanors. His manifest persona he had adopted as a tattooist was brash, rude and cruel. It was too tempting for the base- level earth persona to carry on being abusive, it was more fun and it gave him more credibility with his peers. I saw that credibility had always mattered to him, in the past-life he sought my fathers accolades above his friends loyalty.

166

In this life he desired to be seen as a swaggering and wealthy womaniser. In fact the soul beneath the guise seemed damaged and insecure, it was to the soul I had to appeal.

Psychic action: In meditation I 're-enacted' the past-life scenario in my mind's-eye, With psychic vision I became my previous character and Mark became his. I did this as I knew his current persona was built up around his soul so strongly that I needed to go back to before the soul damage was inflicted. I talked to the soul as it was in that life, before it had made the choice to 'grass' on my lover. I did not try to convince him otherwise but I did explain the debt he would owe to me and the lover if he made the soul-connection that he was choosing to.

Murder is a strong link, even 'indirect' murder. I suggested that his soul may care to 'let me go' by behaving decently to me so that no further meetings would be required. I asked for a severing of ties between us, I could forgive him if he chose to do the right thing by myself and my lover. In 'the now' Mark and I had made a deal for him to teach me tattooing. I needed this to be completed adequately and to be treated respectfully with no further abuse. The soul of Mark could think about what I had said and decide for himself, it was in his hands.

Result of psychic interaction: The choice Mark made was to go with the peer admiration and financial rewards. Therefore he chose to still be disloyal to my lover and, in this life, to still treat me like a fool for the benefit of his friends. His soul lost out against the more powerful will of his current personality. I could see, in further psychic impressions, many lifetimes of his being tempted away from his soul's purpose by riches or women who made him seem more impressive than he was. I saw a twisted and damaged soul and I tried to do some healing with it without interfering with it too greatly.

Conclusion: I have cut all my psychic ties to Mark and have no desire to meet him again. He, however, is still in soul-debt to me. He did choose to end the scenario as well as he could but he still left me short-changed from my tattoo training. Having contacted my soul and that of my partner in order to recompense for his last 'cock up' he was responsible for 'summoning' two independent souls. As he had then proceeded to continue to 'cock up' then he has deepened his debt. By his summoning of us he affected the patterns of the souls for no positive purpose. On a personal soul-level and on a level of the All, Mark will one day, one incarnation, have to make amends.

Note: Mark is not an evil person. He is not my enemy, I do not hate him. Psychism and Wildwitchery gives me the perspective to see the whole story to the best of my ability. Mark is a damaged soul. I wish healing for him, that is all. I demand no revenge or any retribution. I require no further tie with his soul. I hope that one day that small, eternal part of him may better find expression incarnate. It is sad to witness someone so ill at ease with themselves on all levels.

All my soul, or my partner's soul, ever required of his was respect and kindness. May we all learn, as part of the All and so connected to the soul of Mark, from his mistakes.

Case Two. The Problem of an Energy Block

Name: Cee

Relation to myself: friend

Nature of the problem: Cee could not achieve promotion within her field of work although she was convinced that she was good enough. Cee's partner had several affairs whilst Cee was dealing with her professional difficulties. Cee's partner then got a job abroad whilst Cee ended up in a shared student accommodation.

Energies involved: Cee's soul had old wounds opened up by the trauma of her partner's infidelity. In her desire to achieve at work, she placed great store in maintaining a controlled professional image. Any feelings unleashed by the trauma were firmly quashed and controlled for the benefit of her work persona. Cee's soul was feeling pain, hurt, fear and anger whilst her manifest self was rigidly attempting to be a modern, successful woman. Cee's key word was control.

Any other factors: The house that Cee moved into was occupied by a spiritually inclined woman who befriended Cee. Cee initially rejected the woman as being 'not her type' (i.e. Cee was a career go getter with aspirations for herself, the house-mate was more artistic, literary and 'hippy-ish'). Gradually, the efforts of the spiritual woman, combined with Cee's increasing loneliness and unhappiness meant that Cee went along to a few workshops with her house-mate. Cee found that she enjoyed the lectures and groups on some level and became interested in the subject matter herself. This interest did not go down well with the professional persona who remained in control. An inner conflict began in which the newly awakened spiritual/feeling side of Cee battled for space with the controlled career woman. Cee spent the next year going nowhere with her work, being turned down for jobs and becoming increasingly unhappy.

Psychic diagnosis: The disharmony created within Cee was a direct result of her conflict between her long-held material aspirations and her less secure, scary inner feelings. The spiritual path seemed more satisfying but Cee did not know how to let go of her dream of being a glamourous professional climbing the career ladder with a successful husband, own home and expensive new car.

169

With Cee's permission I went into meditation to speak to her soul (or higher) self. The soul showed me the current Cee persona as being like a child in a tantrum, a child which had thought it was their right to have material success and the modern dream lifestyle. Further questioning revealed that Cee's soul had been incarnate at the time of the French revolution and it had enjoyed the life of a pampered aristocrat, thank you very much! The energies of "I want, I shall have now!" were still strong and resonant for her soul.

However, the energies of spiritual fulfilment also came into the equation. For this, Cee's soul revealed it had been incarnate in South America after that French life of indulgence. Her soul had chosen the life of a peasant there as a counterbalance to the excess of aristocratic existence. She had enjoyed the simplicity of a peasant's earthy, natural connection too.

Somehow her soul's memory of its liking for indulging the material side of being had been triggered by Cee's present upbringing and circumstance, not to mention modern societies' mores. Her having been forced to enter a shared house and meet the spiritual woman was enough to trigger the 'peasant response', the affinity with the simple and sacred. Cee's soul was in conflict as her incarnate self would not relinquish control and go with the new energies. There was a way to unite these aspects if she could let go.

Psychic action: Having gained these insights from Cee's own soul I recommended to her that she went with the flow. If she did not then her soul would force her manifest self to stop, it would force her to let go and relinquish control so that the new energies may re-align her way of being. Consequently Cee's outlook and priorities would change and she would not be so dominated by the need to get on and succeed.

170

Result of Psychic Interaction: Cee refused to acknowledge the guidance. It did not provide an instant answer to how she may gain promotion. She still thought that this was the only thing that would truly make her happy. She thought that she had been wasting her time on all that spiritual rubbish. She threw herself into her work more intensely than ever. Cee's soul had no choice but to physically make her stop. She suffered with a terrible case of appendicitis which resulted in her being immobile and in a state of contemplation for many weeks afterwards.

The soul took the only option left open to it and Cee was duly made to let go of her tight controls and feel not only the physical pain but also her long-held emotional grief and rage. All that festering emotion was symbolically made manifest in her illness although it had been making her spirit ill for some time. Cee had to admit that there was more to her Self than the surface level. She needed to get in touch with those neglected aspects of spirit that she had not cared for.

Conclusion: Cee had to be helped to re-integrate these rejected and sick aspects of her being. She had to re-align her passion for the material with her acceptance of the spiritual. Hardest of all, she had to go with the flow. Her Guide was asked to step in and help with the process.

Note: Cee should not have been so hard on herself. She needed healing and lots of encouragement. Her own exacting standards had been impossible, idealistic goals for herself. Since abandoning these unachievable targets for herself, Cee has got a new job with less stress and which is more rewarding to her soul. The pay stayed the same but Cee was no longer focussed upon money so exclusively. She now values her work on how worthwhile it is, rather than how prestigious. Cee values her free time and social interactions much more. Her spirituality has found an outlet and is a quiet counterpoint to her daily way of life.

Case Three The Problem of Unwanted Magic

Name: Myself.

Nature of the problem: Marilyn is an adept psychic. When she focuses her will upon me it is with formidable force. She is of the opinion that such attentions are because she loves me and wishes the best for me. However, with the best will in the world, her ideas are not my own.

Part of her plan for me is to find me a 'suitable' partner. Having mentioned a male friend that she liked the sound of she decided to put a bit of focus in...hence my male friend suddenly became rather enamoured of me...

Energies involved: My own psychic understanding, Marilyn's lack of understanding but enormous psychic will, my male friend's loneliness and vulnerability as a target.

Any other factors: I had told Marilyn of my friend recently ending his relationship. My friend was close to me at this time confiding his emotional woes. I was attuned to his spirit more than I was usually. Marilyn heard more about him than usual due to my closer involvement at his time of need.

Psychic Diagnosis: It did not need much astral 'peering' to see that Marilyn had psychically bound or corded myself and my friend together on the astral levels. She had done this by her intense wish and will for me to have an 'appropriate' (In her eyes) partner. This was a strong need in her and so the cords were strong too.

Psychic Action: I had to remove the astral cords between us one by one, methodically perusing the astral bodies until all cords were severed. I had to repeat this exercise until I was satisfied that Marilyn's attentions had lapsed. I also had to physically and manifestly break the close links with the friend, I could not see him for a while.

Result of psychic interaction: One very bemused friend. I did not hurt him in any way but he was confused as to a) why he had suddenly felt so enamoured of me out of the blue and b) why I would not see him.

Conclusion: It is not good to do anything to anyone psychically without their consent. Marilyn is a natural but untrained psychic. She does not know any better than to think that if she thinks she is acting for the good, then it is ok. The moral of this case is, do not ever assume an act of astral interference is reasonable if you yourself deem it to be for the good. My friendship with this man is probably permanently damaged and he has been caused unnecessary confusion.

Also, never underestimate the power of thought, wish and will. This is your magic, your spell-making and your power as a Wildwitch. Do not abuse it, even 'for the good'.

In summary, my advice would be as follows,

The Way of the Wildwitch:
1. Know your Guide, always check any procedure with them. Achieve a full working relationship with the Otherworlds through them.

2. Practice astral protection at all times.

3. Know yourself, do not be afraid to learn, grow and change.

4. Appreciate your soul as an integral part of the All. Accept that we are one another, interwoven and connected.

5. Know that everything is energies, our energies are everything. We can affect change.

6. Know that we do not know. Our truths are personal ones subject to change, they are not universal absolutes.

7. Learn to forgive and to love based on the premise that we too may be the slave, the murderer or the child-abuser. None of us are 'above' anything. Our souls use many masks to learn by. We all have many lives, many selves.

8. Be proud of the psychic gift and strive to be a shining representative of the Wild Ways.

9. Help others with humility and strength through the gifts we have.

10. Have reverence for the natural world of which we are a part. Treat it with awe, behold it with joy, dance the sacred, secret dances daily. Find your stars, find your own unique and personal vision-path.

Conclusion

Shine!

In conclusion I will share with you some guidance I received recently as regards my role 'in the World' as a Wildwitch. The piece is paraphrased as some of it is personal but the general feeling is expressed.

"There is no need to hide from people. Shine! There is no need to take on the value judgements of others and to hide away because of them. Be proud but not vain. Do not judge or be bigoted but stand proud at all times. The true path is with the self, self knowledge. For your self you know that you belong to another race. You are truly out of time and place but you will meet others, there are others like yourself. Your role is to speak from the soul with love and care, this is the language of your race.

How will these others recognise you and each other if you hide your individual lights? There will be no recognition if you are afraid, no unity. No one can really hurt you now and could they ever? For here you are again, elf-arrow flying free. Be at peace with yourself and others and do not perish in these environs. There is a place here for you to grow freely. You can reach out now and you need never give up. You cannot die if you keep the faith. Let go, let Goddess! The gift of your race is love, love enough to heal. Healing through contact with us, the Otherworlds, each other, the self...the All.

Believe this, you are safe to walk your own path. Waste no more time trying to compete with other races and look forwards on your own track. You have much to give. The

sacrifice of your race is an ever open door. Welcome people and accept them without judgement as you too deserve acceptance. Love and heal them. There is no more than this. Shine!"

I was born into this world with the Seeing and the Knowing. I am wild and proud and free.

So may you be.

Wildwitch

Shells and Bells and Cones and Stones
I feel it in my Blood and Bones
I of the Sea, I of the Land
Sorcery is in my Hands
Magic born of Power Mine
My Energy and yours entwine
Fire in the Belly, Fire in the Eyes
A Wildwitch under Starlit Skies
To mend, to tend, to bend, to love
As it is Below and so Above
A Dream, a Dance, a Song well sung
If you follow me you'll hear it wrong
Breeze blow, Grass grow, Feather fall
Go your own way, part of the All
Wild Wood, Wild Blood, Moon and Star
Wildwitch loved for What You Are
Wildwitch loved for Who I Be
I'll hold your Hand, you're Part of Me
Shells and Bells and Cones and Stones
I feel you in my Blood and Bones.

A selection of other Capall Bann titles. Free catalogue available.

Season of Sorcery- On Becoming a Wisewoman by Poppy Palin

Many people experience psychic phenomena to a greater or lesser degree, depending on their own innate sensitivity. Such experiences can cause delight or distress and can be difficult to share with others. This book is a personal story of psychic encounters, and the author's own understanding of them, presented as a fascinating blend of information and entertainment. In sharing her own unusual experiences, the author hopes to encourage others to gain knowledge and understanding of their own. The book therefore seeks to inspire by revealing the author's own practical understanding and enjoyment or her own psychism and encouraging the reader to develop and understand their own. ISBN 1898307 96 2   £10.95

Psychic Self Defence - Real Solutions by Jan Brodie

How to recognise a psychic attack & how to handle it? This book concentrates on a commonsense approach to problems including interviews describing how people have dealt with attacks. Practical information, based on real experiences, is given on a range of protective & self development measures:- Summoning a guardian. Coping with psychic attack during magical or circle work, Banishing 'evil' influences, Holding your own in the Otherworlds/Astral levels. Protective amulets & talismans, Strengthening the aura, Avoiding the pitfalls on the occult path, Increasing self-confidence in magical work & visualisation, Psychic attack - What it is & What it is not, Elemental Spirits of Nature, Guardian Spirits, the Aura, the Astral Levels, the Psychic Vampire, the Realm of Faerie, Ghosts, Psychic Attack Through Willpower & the Evil Eye. *"very readable, sensible...clear and reassuring...recommended" Pagan Dawn.* ISBN 1898307 36 9   £8.95

Between Earth and Sky by Julia Day

Julia is a member of a Celtic Tradition. "I believe that whatever our beliefs or Tradition, we each make and follow our own path. I hope this book may help you to follow yours." *"Between Earth and Sky"* is a collection of articles, environmental reports, thoughts, visualisations, poems and stories, together with inspired writings which may help the reader to explore their own thoughts and feelings in many areas of magical, Pagan life."We are seeking to reconcile the physical world and spirit, the Earth and the Sky, just as we have always done. Earth below and Sky above. It is in that tension between the two that we learn and develop. As with the active and passive principle, the instrument of fertilisation and that which is made fertile, Male and Female, it is within that tension, that both the religion and our own development remains alive." ISBN 186163 0506   £9.95

Patchwork of Magic - Living In a Pagan World by Julia Day

This book contains many experiences, facts, thoughts and ideas. It has a light-hearted look at Pagan life and compares subdivisions which have formed within that world, groups as diverse as Druids and Chaos workers. Includes making incense, magic during everyday activities, initiation, help with personal development, grounding, centring, learning from dreams, recognising synchronicity and living an increasingly magical life. This book combines the natural energies of Earth and Sky, sewn together with love and laughter. *"....wise counsel based on personal experience...should be required reading. Highly recommended." The Cauldron. ".....extremely funny...beautifully trashes the pretentious....clear and sane, totally grounded....rich in common sense." OBOD Touchstone.* ISBN 1898 307210   £9.95

FREE DETAILED CATALOGUE

A detailed illustrated catalogue is available on request, SAE or International Postal Coupon appreciated. **Titles can be ordered direct from Capall Bann, post free in the UK** (cheque or PO with order) or from good bookshops and specialist outlets. Titles currently available include:

Auguries and Omens - The Magical Lore of Birds by Yvonne Aburrow
Caer Sidhe - Celtic Astrology and Astronomy by Michael Bayley
Call of the Horned Piper by Nigel Jackson
Celtic Lore & Druidic Ritual by Rhiannon Ryall
Earth Dance - A Year of Pagan Rituals by Jan Brodie
Earth Magic by Margaret McArthur
Enchanted Forest - The Magical Lore of Trees by Yvonne Aburrow
Familiars - Animal Powers of Britain by Anna Franklin
Healing Book (The) by Chris Thomas
Handbook For Pagan Healers by Liz Joan
Healing Homes by Jennifer Dent
Herbcraft - Shamanic & Ritual Use of Herbs by S Lavender & A Franklin
In Search of Herne the Hunter by Eric Fitch
Magical Guardians - Exploring the Spirit & Nature of Trees by P Heselton
Magical Lore of Cats by Marion Davies
Magical Lore of Herbs by Marion Davies
Patchwork of Magic by Julia Day
Psychic Self Defence - Real Solutions by Jan Brodie
Sacred Animals by Gordon MacLellan
Sacred Grove - The Mysteries of the Forest by Yvonne Aburrow
Sacred Geometry by Nigel Pennick
Sacred Lore of Horses The by Marion Davies
Secret Places of the Goddess by Philip Heselton
Talking to the Earth by Gordon Maclellan

Capall Bann is owned and run by people actively involved in many of the areas in which we publish. Our list is expanding rapidly so do contact us for details on the latest releases.

Capall Bann Publishing, Freshfields, Chieveley, Berks, RG20 8TF